Spiritual Gardening

Spiritual Gardening

CREATING SACRED SPACE OUTDOORS

by Peg Streep

Principal Photography by John Glover

TIME LIFE BOOKS

Alexandria, Virginia

Time-Life Books is a division of Time Life Inc.

TIME LIFE INC.
PRESIDENT and CEO: George Artandi

TIME-LIFE CUSTOM PUBLISHING
Vice President and Publisher: Terry Newell
Vice President of Sales and Marketing: Neil Levin
Director of Acquisitions and Editorial Resources: Jennifer Pearce
Editor for Special Markets: Anna Marlis Burgard
Director of Creative Services: Laura McNeill

Prepared and produced by Layla Productions, Inc., NY
Project Director: Lori Stein
Editor: Leslie Garisto
Designer: Annemarie Redmond
Spiritual Advisor: Alexandra E. Israel
Artistic Consultant: Lily E. Pfaff
Support Staff: Johanna M. Gregory
Technical Guru: Michelle Stein
Financial Services: Deena Stein

Library of Congress Cataloging-in-Publication Data

Streep, Peg
Spiritual gardening : creating sacred space outdoors / by Peg Streep
p.   cm.
Includes bibliographical references (p.   ) and index.
ISBN: 0-7370-0060-0 (hardcover)
ISBN: 0-7370-0074-0 (softcover)
1. Gardens. 2. Gardening. 3. Gardens—Religious aspects.
4. Gardening—Religious aspects. I. Time-Life Books. II. Title.
SB455.S817   1999
635'.01—dc21   99-15243 CIP

Printed in China

First printing 1999

1 2 3 4 5 6 7 8 9   99 00 01 02 03 04 05

NOTE: Readers are advised to be aware that some of the plants mentioned in this book have toxic, carcinogenic, or other dangerous properties. No remedies mentioned in this book should be taken as medications without proper medical advice and no plant should ever be taken internally or used near food unless it is determined to be totally safe. Special care should be taken if children or pets frequent the areas where these plants are grown.

Although all the information in this book has been carefully researched, the author, editors, and publishers assume no responsibility for any injuries suffered or for damages or losses incurred due to following information in this book.

For photo credits and acknowledgments, see page 191.

Books produced by Time-Life Custom Publishing are available
at special bulk discount for promotional and premium use.
Custom adaptations can also be created to meet your specific marketing goals.
Call 1-800-323-5255.

For Alexandra,

whose soul is a garden in flower

Contents

I. GARDENING FOR THE SOUL 8

II. THE SPIRITUAL GARDENS 74

The Tranquillity Garden 78

The Healing Garden 88

The Zen Garden 98

The Gaia Garden 112

The Aromatherapy Garden 122

The Feng Shui Garden 130

The Celtic Garden 138

The Biblical Garden 144

The Saint's Garden 150

The Labyrinth Garden 156

III. GARDENING AS A SPIRITUAL EXERCISE 164

Sources 180

Selected Bibliography 185

Index 187

Sources for Quotation 191

Garden Design Credits 191

Illustration credits 191

Acknowledgments 192

Gardening for the Soul

More than anything else, a garden is a portal,
a passage into another world, one of your own
thoughts and your own making; it is whatever you
want it to be and you are what you want to be.

William Longgood

On Creating Sacred Space

We transform our gardens and yards into sacred space when we understand them as places of growth not only for plants and trees but for our inner selves. What is "sacred" space? It is a place of dedication, where the miracles of life and growth are acknowledged as evidence of something larger than ourselves. That "something larger" can be called by many different names, and may refer to the presence of a specific deity, a unifying or supernatural pattern, or simply our membership in the great community of living organisms—the discovered 1,413,000 separate species—that populate the planet Earth. With understanding and acknowledgment, we can turn our own gardens into places of sanctuary. The Latin word for "sacred" gives us the word "sanctuary," denoting not only a sacred space but also a place of refuge and protection. The garden can become a place where we can restore our emotional and spiritual balance and nourish our senses and souls, away from the noise of everyday life.

Gardening is a vehicle for spiritual and emotional connection. It is, when you think about it, nothing short of miraculous: You kneel, dig a bit, drop in a seed, add water, and wait. In time the miracle unveils itself, beginning with an ever-so-tentative shoot of green: Life! It is, perhaps, not as dramatic as being witness to the

Everything that slows us down and forces patience, everything that sets us back into the slow cycles of nature, is a help. Gardening is an instrument of grace.

May Sarton

creation of the universe or even that moment when a single sperm pierces the shell of the human ovum, but for most of us it is as close as we will ever get to witnessing a miracle firsthand.

This deceptively simple yet completely extraordinary event lies at the very heart of gardening. It alone explains why so many of us feel emotionally sustained by our gardens as we work to sustain the life growing within them. The small miracle hints at why gardening is so much more than a hobby (albeit America's favorite hobby) and why the garden is so much more than just another "room" to be decorated. Gardening lets us participate in the process that is life, from the greening of the shoot to the dying-off of the flower. The planning and the imagining of the garden—from poring through seed catalogs to eyeing the plants in a nursery to designing the layout of beds and space—make us co-creators

Above: *At the Institute for American Indian Studies, simple tree stumps become welcoming places to contemplate the medicine wheel garden.*

Opposite left: *Calm suffuses this Oriental-style garden at the Penick residence in Virginia.*

Opposite right: *The tiniest of details, a small statue of Buddha, creates sacred space.*

Opposite bottom: *The labyrinth seems to rise out of the earth and embody its spirit.*

with nature and, in a true sense, realizers of potential. There is something "heartening" about growing a plant from seed and seeing it flower, or eating a tomato grown on your own vine. For most of us, too, the time we spend in the garden constitutes our main life-line to the natural world.

Creating sacred space moves us beyond mere decorating in the outdoors. When we garden for the soul, we use the experiences in the garden to tend our inner landscapes and foster the growth of spirit. In the spiritual garden, with the miracle in mind, we consciously and deliberately restore the meaning and symbolic intent of what might otherwise be considered ordinary tasks: digging, planting, watering, tending and maintaining the outer landscape.

The religious and spiritual traditions represented in the many gardens described and pictured on the pages that follow are drawn from all over the world and are, in some respects, markedly different from one another. They offer a host of alternatives to the "how" of creating sacred space outdoors, although they share in common the "why." Each of them understands the garden as a place where we can go not to admire our skill as gardeners but to come into contact with the spiritual essence of nature—whether that is the hand of the Creator or Creatrix, or the amazing riches of a biodiverse world. They share the goal of helping us—as seekers and as gardeners—live more meaningful and dedicated lives, enriched by spirit.

GARDENING AS A SPIRITUAL TOOL

We don't know precisely when the first human being planted a seed and became an active participant in the mystery and magic of the cycle of nature, capable of transforming the landscape. We don't even know how this knowledge, which ultimately would change the course of human history, was acquired. In a quiet moment we wonder: Was it gleaned or wrested from the earth? Was it simply a matter of the observant eye: watching the pod fall unaided from the plant and insinuating itself into the soil, only to grow up as if by a miracle? Or was it an accident: the seed gathered and then scattered by human hands, flourishing months later, the germ of the idea vivid in the mind? Was it patience and belief set to the rhythm of failure and success: bits of the flower, fruit, or plant harvested and then the slow waiting, time and again, generation after generation?

The discovery of planting was probably born of need but it couldn't have been long before the first gardeners, over 10,000 years ago, recognized that more than just the hunger in their bellies was being fed. We know that, in time, the storytellers acknowledged the mysterious forces that gave them the gifts of seed and plant, of earth and water, the cycles of the seasons, and of the moon and sun. Humans gave these forces names and forms, and offered them thanks. These ancient but once-sacred stories—preserved for us only as statues of now-nameless grain goddesses—are lost to us, but later sacred stories—of the Egyptian Isis and Osiris, the Greek Demeter, or the Native American Changing Woman—remind us that humanity has always understood the provenance of earth's gifts as sacral in nature.

Understanding the awesome power of the seed—its literal and symbolic promise of renewal—changed both how human beings lived on the face of the earth and their spiritual understanding. Sowing the seed permitted them to settle, farm, and claim land as their own. This knowledge altered for many—though not all at once—what had always been the rhythm of human life, shaped by the constant search for new sources of forage and food. The symbolic meaning of the seed—the ever-renewing cycle of nature—changed the human spiritual vision of the cycle of life and death as it affected each individual. From the Neolithic onward, seasonal renewal—the reseeding of earth—became a potent metaphor for human resurrection, reflected in the much later custom of the ancient Greeks, who kept a pot of seeds representing the household's dead near the hearth.

The cycle of nature—the progress from seed to fruition to dying-off and then renewal in the spring—was mirrored in the wild fields and the cultivated garden alike, while the fragility of harvest—the possible interruption of the cycle by drought, wind, or other natural calamities—established the pattern of how humans understood the workings of the cosmos. The oldest of surviving sacred stories have their roots in the garden and reflect how humanity sought to understand the changeable patterns of their world and, at the same time, to imagine a world no longer subject to change. It's no accident that our own word "paradise" comes from a Persian word for an enclosed garden.

It took thousands of years from the first cultivation of seeds to the earliest creation of what we call a garden—an enclosed place of cultivation, rather than a field—and even then the earliest gardens recorded still reflected the sacral nature of planting. Gardens in ancient Egypt were often located near both tombs and temples, suggesting that the gardens, as well as the plants grown within them, served both funerary and religious purposes. Gardens, like the temples, honored the gods. And even as they performed secular functions such as displaying wealth, providing pleasure, and even testifying to the power that was Egypt (the booty of armies included the indigenous plants and shrubs of conquered lands), the cultivated flowers ands shrubs grown in these gardens were also used for religious purposes. Similarly, in ancient Mesopotamia, even though walled garden were sites of pleasure— Assurbanipal and his wife are depicted feasting in their garden in a seventh-century B.C. relief—they were also understood as places of sanctuary and the source of the flowers and leaves used in daily worship of the gods. In ancient Greece the uncultivated sacred grove of trees coexisted with courtyard gardens sacred to Adonis and

Nature preaches a lesson in renewal: the seed bursting through the soil (opposite) and then the poppy, itself a symbol of resurrection, first in bud (above) and then as seed head (left).

public parks in which statues of the gods and goddesses testified to the sacrality of cultivated outdoor space. Even though the Romans secularized the garden and invented the idea of the garden as an exterior "room"—horticulture for the Romans was, in many instances, purely ornamental and a testament to pleasure and wealth—the gods were still felt to be present in the gardens where their floral offerings were grown.

The rebirth of "civilization" called the Renaissance marked the triumph of the secular in the garden and the displacement of the spiritual (outside of those gardens cultivated by members of religious communities). Human artistry was celebrated in the garden's design and details; beauty and comfort were its primary objectives. And while the miracle of life still took place in the garden, outdoor space was, first and foremost, a reflection of its owner. Nowhere is this more evident than in the grandeur of seventeenth-century Versailles, perhaps, in terms of the influence of its garden design, one of the most significant gardens ever created.

Rediscovering "gardening as an instrument of grace," to use May Sarton's words, requires that we go back in time to recover our sense of wonder. Much separates us from those who discovered the power of

the seed but now, thousands of years later at the dawn of a new millennium, more and more of us are experiencing the sense of spirit our ancestors on the planet acknowledged in the soil beneath their feet and in the seed itself. Gardening engages all five of the human senses as few activities do. We see, smell, feel, hear, and even taste as we gar-

Above: *Gardening allows us to pause in the midst of our overloaded modern lives and see the hidden details of our surroundings. Here, a blue poppy* (Meconopsis betonicifolia) *reveals its bright, sunlike center.*

Opposite: *The complexity of the natural world is captured in a single, extraordinary detail: a western trillium reflected in a raindrop.*

den, and, because all of our senses are involved, what we experience is vivid and specific. The simple acts of gardening—digging, tamping, working the dirt, and watering—have echoes that reach back to childhood, whether we played in the suburbs or in a city park. As we garden we experience time past and present. Touching the earth—digging, planting, harvesting—connects us literally and spiritually to all those who have dug, planted, and harvested before us. Working in the garden permits us to begin to understand the woven pattern of relationships in nature, and teaches us that nothing in nature is either independent or isolated.

When we garden we reconnect ourselves to the slow rhythms of the cosmos. Our knees in the dirt, our faces close to the ground, we dig in the soil and see the myriad forms of life hidden to us when we are upright and walking: the earthworm tunneling through the soil, the outlined whiteness of the grub, the sticky trail of the slug. The perfumes of the garden—the rich loamy smell of water-laden soil or the acrid bite of the geranium—revive us and remind us that the world has a palette of scent as well as color. The sweetness of a berry and the cool note of mint encompass a range of taste and feeling, and teach a lesson in opposites. We breathe deep as our fingers work the soil, and marvel at the texture of the visible world: the soft fuzz of a begonia's leaf, the pansy's fragile velvet, the feathery lightness of dill. And then there is the music of a garden, set apart from the noise-filled world in which we usually live: the evening call of the summer cicada or the whisper of grasses, the crackle of fallen leaves underfoot.

Gardening also helps us come to terms with the cycle of human life. Many of us tend to see our lives as linear, moving from points A to B in progression, with birth and death at opposite ends of the continuum, but the garden teaches another lesson entirely. In nature, beginnings and endings, birth and death, are inseparable: implicit in the flower's blooming is its dying-off as well as its eventual renewal. The perennials in our winter garden—dead aboveground, still awake below—teach us about time and hidden mysteries. The withered annual is a symbol of the

larger pattern that extends beyond us and our gardens: Seeds borne by the wind and birds bring small pieces of our lives into other places and other lives, making new, if unseen, connections. Planting seeds makes us active participants in the cycle of life, while tending our gardens teaches us about larger patterns of the cycle that are beyond our control. We learn patience from the long wait from planting to sprouting to blooming, as we learn acceptance when nature takes its own course. We gain humility when we catch a true glimpse of the extraordinary complexity of the natural world.

With all of our senses engaged, seeing becomes understanding in the garden. Just as the medieval monks could see God's presence in His handiwork and could make it the starting point for a meditation, so, too, we are learning to go into the garden to glimpse the "larger pattern"—

regardless of what we name it—which seems to elude us in the other details of our everyday lives. This book was written and designed so that these experiences could be shared; our lives are enriched when we understand that the seeds in our hands are the promise of tomorrow.

THE SACRALITY OF NATURE

For thousands of years human beings understood the visible world of nature to be a manifestation of a supernatural presence. Physical places—mountaintops and peaks, caverns deep in the earth, stands of trees, bodies of water—were thought to be inherently sacred and indicative of a deity's proximity by virtue of their beauty, splendor, or mystery. The physical world was, by definition, a locus for spirit which was to be glimpsed everywhere, and the landscape was understood as symbolic of a larger supernatural truth. Gods and goddesses were worshiped outdoors by the ancient Minoans, Egyptians, Greeks, Romans, and Celts; a temple only housed effigies of a deity—it was the deity's home—and wasn't intended for public worship. Natural epiphanies of the deities—rocks, specific trees, gorges, flowers—defined outside space as sacred and symbolic.

The Judeo-Christian tradition changed the Western understanding of the landscape in more ways than one. According to the Book of Genesis, God first planted a garden and then created Adam and Eve to live within it in perfect harmony with all their surroundings. With their disobedience and expulsion from Eden, the natural landscape of the post-Edenic world, fallen from grace, became profane, not sacred, and humanity's relationship to it forever changed. Yet as both the Old and the New

Opposite: *Standing stones, thousands of years old, dot the landscape of France and England, delineating precincts once recognized by humanity as sacred.*

Above right: *Glastonbury in England has sacral associations that predate Christianity and are reflected in Arthurian stories. Legend has it that St. Joseph of Arimaethea founded England's first Christian church here; it was said, too, that when the saint rested his staff on Wearyall Hill, it rooted and became the Glastonbury thorn that blooms on Christmas Eve. In the Middle Ages, it was an important place of pilgrimage.*

Right: *Ancient petroglyphs in New Mexico, a testament to the sacred landscape.*

There is life
in the ground;
it goes into the seeds;
and it also goes
into the man
who stirs it.

Charles Dudley Warner

Testaments show, the metaphors of the natural world and the garden remained the primary vocabulary to describe both God's presence and the role of the spirit in human life. In Jeremiah the planted garden becomes a symbol of enduring faith; in Isaiah the planting of cultivated trees in the wilderness is the emblem of God's all-present majesty and power. In Psalms the righteous man is "like a tree planted by the rivers of water, that bringeth forth his fruit in his season; his life also shall not wither." Two of the

Above: *Half-hidden by the sago palm's fronds, a small stone tower or pagoda, nestled on moss, is a visual reminder of a deity's presence.*

events central to the story of Jesus and the Christian faith take place in cultivated space, the Garden of Gethsemane and the garden where he is laid in a new sepulchre by Joseph of Arimathea and Nicodemus and where, in a spiritually important metaphor, the resurrected Christ is mistaken for a gardener by Mary Magdalene. In the later Christian tradition, the garden—particularly the walled garden separate from the outside world—became a symbol of that first paradise lost as well as a prefiguration of the new paradise promised, heaven.

Other traditions can be brought to bear on contemporary spiritual gardening to help reinvigorate our

understanding of the landscape as sacred. The Native American spiritual vision, which has been culturally influential as a rediscovered model in recent decades, is based on the oneness of all existing things; humanity is not set apart from the cosmos but is indistinguishable from it. The spiritual was perceived visible in the animate and the inanimate alike; all the parts of creation—trees, plants, animals, stones, even humanity itself—were equal as the children of Mother Earth and Father Sky. The cycles of time, too, were part of all that existed, and bound all things together in what was understood as a sacred circle or web. The Native American model is one of interconnectedness and reciprocity. For each gift contained in the natural world—whether the nourishment of corn, the coming of rain, or the plenty of game—humanity honored

its source and gave thanks. In this vision of the sacred, humanity was understood as an active participant in the universe's magic and mystery. Ritual, song, dance, and the making of offerings assured the continuance of the cycles of growth, death, and rebirth in the sun's and moon's rising and setting, the planting and harvesting of the crops, and the birth and death of each individual. All of life was ceremonial in nature; for the Native American peoples what we understand as the distinction between the ordinary and the sacred simply did not exist.

Another vision of the sacred landscape, one that yielded the Taoist garden, comes to us from the Orient. At the very center of this tradition is a different view of the universe that is also holistic and based on interrelation. All living things are connected by cosmic energy or *chi*, and chi itself is made up of the opposing forces of *yin* and *yang*. Feng shui, an ancient Chinese art, is intimately connected in its history to the landscape, even though its most popular application in the United States has been to interior space. Over the centuries the principles of feng shui developed

from observation based in humanity's necessary relationship and dependence on nature. Learning to live in balance with nature by adjusting for the forces of yin and yang is the basis for feng shui; practically it means working with the natural energy of the landscape rather than against it (such as building houses that face south to maximize the heat of sun or on hillsides to minimize loss from

Above: *In the tradition of the Japanese tea garden, the lantern is a symbol of sacred space, its rounded top an emblem of the lotus bud.*

floods as well as danger from hostile invaders). This vision of nature is neither judgmental nor moralistic (neither yin nor yang is either "good" or "bad") but essentially descriptive. In this system, the natural world—its colors, its elements, its cardinal points, its energies—provides the model for living with balance. (For more, see "The Feng Shui Garden," page 130.)

A much more stylized and symbolic vision of landscape is that of the Zen garden. Its symbolism has its roots in the Shinto religion, which was animistic in its view of nature and landscape, and which honored both the ancestors and nature spirits thought to live in specific rocks and stones. Set apart by specially woven straw ropes, these rocks in a Zen garden are honored as sacred precincts. The Shinto legacy is evident in the dry landscape of the Zen garden which, with its symbolic placement of stones and raked patterns of gravel or sand, offers a vision of the natural world defined by Buddhist cosmology or events in the Buddha's life. Zen gardens embody a vision of landscape that alludes to symbolic meaning on every level.

The understanding of the landscape as symbolically meaningful and sacred in nature underlies every spiritual garden.

CREATING SACRED SPACE OUTDOORS

In contemporary times the idea of the garden as sacred space—a place where, as Joseph Campbell put it, "wonder can be revealed"—can draw on many varied traditions. Designed as places where the soul can be fed and the mind can be soothed, spiritual gardens use different vocabularies of design but all share a basic characteristic: They treat the elements of landscape design as allusions to a larger truth or revelation of principle. In the Zen garden the close relationship of a few carefully chosen natural elements reveals the harmony implicit in nature; in the Gaia garden the planting of wildflowers alludes to

Above: *Stone guardians mark the entrance to sacred space, here in the inner courtyard of the Korean ambassador's garden in Washington, D.C.*

both the fragility and sustainability of the planet we live on. In the spiritual garden, the presence of the divine can be indicated by statuary, whether that of the Virgin Mary or the Buddha; the sacred can be invoked by using symbolic elements such as spirals and circles; the spiritual journey that is life can be signified by gates or pathways.

A spiritual garden can be a sanctuary or retreat for meditation, a place to celebrate earth in all of its majesty, or a source for and inspiration to healing. Gardening is both a creative and a physical activity, one that draws on the intellect and the emotions, the conscious and the unconscious. Over the course of time both your spiritual intention and your use of sacred space outdoors may change as the act of gardening and the garden itself transform your spirit.

Diane, a musician who lives on the ground floor of a house in a small eastern city, didn't consciously set out to create a spiritual garden when she moved to her apartment five years ago. She saw possibilities in the brick-walled yard—some 20 feet deep and 12 feet wide—even though the previous tenants had done little with it. Diane decided that what she wanted to create was a small oasis that would add beauty to the urban environment. For the first few years she experimented with shade-loving plants since there was little sun but, as luck would have it, changes in the surrounding neighborhood—alterations to a building nearby, the removal of ailanthus trees on the street—improved the garden's potential. Slowly, as Diane learned what would thrive in her garden, she added climbing hydrangea (*Hydrangea anomala* 'Petiolaris'), periwinkle (*Vinca minor*), and clematis to grow over the back wall and the latticework of her deck. Because of the limited space, she decided to plant in pots and containers and, because of the shallow levels of soil, to focus mainly on annuals. In the beginning a small statue of an angel watched over the garden, but several years ago, a single addition—a special gift—began to change the garden's essential nature. The gift was an exquisitely carved Buddha that had belonged to artist and singer Laura Nyro, who died in 1997; at her home

Above right: *The spiritual lesson of humanity's stewardship of the earth is made manifest in this beautiful organic garden.*

Right: *The hand of Buddha shown in the* **Vitarka Mudra**—*the teaching gesture—blesses a courtyard garden in San Francisco, a visual acknowledgment of sacred space.*

Nyro, who followed Buddhist precepts, had kept the statue on a small spit of land off a pond. Diane, who had admired Nyro's work since her girlhood, had been privileged to sing and tour with her during the 1990s. After Nyro's untimely death Diane became close to Nyro's partner, Maria, who gave Diane the Buddha.

The figure of the Buddha, seated on a stone pedestal some two feet tall, has become the spiritual center of Diane's garden. She surrounds it with spiritual objects, such as an incense burner and a pink crystal formation with votive candles which, when lit at night, illuminate both the Buddha's

features and the shadows and shapes of the surrounding plants and flowers. In addition to coleus, impatiens, ferns, and many varieties of hostas, Diane has both day-blooming plants, such as morning glory, and night-blooming ones, including moonflowers and a showy datura. Even when she

Above: *In Diane Garisto's garden, both an angel and a statue of the Buddha watch over the sacred space. In the Buddha's hand is a sprig of lobelia, an offering placed there by Diane.*

Opposite: *Here, in Stephen Huyler's garden, sacred space is deliberately set off from the mundane world by a beautiful stone wall, surrounded by plantings.*

is indoors or away, Diane feels that simply knowing that the garden blooms both day and night elevates her heart and soul to what she calls "another place"; she recalls a favorite saying by Heinrich Heine that "nature is visible thought." Since this spiritual garden is mainly filled by planters, there is no room for naturalizing, but Diane feels that replanting each spring is part of the ritual of renewal. Every autumn she collects seeds from her annuals to replant the following spring. Her spiritual garden is still taking shape; next she intends to build a small fountain out of bluestone salvaged from a building renovation, and to grow scented herbs and plants to elicit "new thoughts" in her urban bower.

Much more consciously planned and much larger in scale is the spiritual garden created and designed by Stephen Huyler, a cultural anthropologist and writer who spends four months each year studying ritual and custom in the rural areas of the Indian subcontinent. Huyler was raised in the mountains of California and Wyoming and lived in Cornwall, England, before moving to Maine. In Cornwall he lived in a house with a garden that had been honored as sacred for centuries: At the edge of the property was an ancient megalithic chamber and 100 acres of woods in which Huyler discovered what might have been a Druidic path. What he calls the dynamic spirit of this garden (and of the many successive generations who respected and enhanced it) has had a profound influence on Huyler's life. When he returned to the United States he looked to his new property in Maine to fill the spiritual void left by his departure from Cornwall.

He was drawn to the one-and-a-quarter-acre property by its three remarkable trees: a mature Japanese maple, an apple tree with an S-curve in its trunk, and the third largest white ash in Maine, 277 years old. The ash, as Huyler notes, is the "grandfather" of the garden, predating the European settlement of what was once Native American land. He envisioned the garden as a series of four "rooms," each of them different; to create them he altered the underlying structure of the existing garden, moving some 500 tons of rock and creating a walled sunken garden, a wooded area, an elevated open garden

with a perennial border and a ledge with a waterfall, and an open wildflower meadow, fully self-seeding. The garden overall has more than 2,000 species of plants.

Huyler consciously chose to see if he could enhance the sacrality of the garden by his commitment, interacting with the plants on a daily basis, and coming into contact with the garden's spirits. He admits that for the first several years, a part of himself was still skeptical about the process—he was acting, as he puts it, "as if"— but in time he has come to recognize the true presence of the spirits around him. In keeping with his work in India,

Above: *The S-curve apple tree in Stephen Huyler's garden. In pagan traditions, the tree and its fruit were sacred, symbolizing knowledge and mystery. For the Greeks, the apple was an emblem of immortality.*

he points out that animism is the belief that everything has its own spirit; when you interact with that spirit, you add something of yourself to it. Over the 14 years he has lived in Maine, Huyler has evolved a daily morning ritual of movement and meditation, beginning in the walled garden where he simply becomes aware and allows himself to be present. In the woods, where he has planted a circle of white birches (representing the groves sacred to ancient civilizations), he sits in the same place each day, on a birch seat made out of a tree trunk, and opens himself to the spirit of each tree.

His daily ritual has been the source for several extraordinary experiences that have taught him, as he puts it, that "the natural world wants to be an active participant in our world and in healing." He recounts how, three years ago, after a full day of writing, he retired to the grove, and his mind turned to the predicament of a mentor who had been afflicted with a devastating case of shingles. In the company of the trees he visualized helping his friend, and received what he describes as a direct message from the trees: "We're here to help." In his vision each plant gave him a thread of a different color, which he then saw as woven into a blanket; Stephen envisioned wrapping it around his mentor's heart, enveloping her heart in color. When he called his mentor to check on her progress, her shingles had disappeared.

While the healing and medicinal properties of plants have been established for thousands of years, more recently the use of gardening as therapy has been recognized by the modern scientific community. (For more see "The Healing Garden," page 88.) Maria Gabaldo, president of the American Association of Horticultural Therapists, points out that as a holistic process—one that combines cognition, creativity, and physical, social, and spiritual activities—gardening has been used as a successful therapeutic tool for the chronically or terminally ill. Because the cycles in the garden mirror those of human life, gardening can help people come to terms with the difficult issues illness presents. Working with plants gives patients a sense of what "rootedness" means, Gabaldo says, while the reemergence of new plants from the debris of the old in the compost pile lends a working analogy to what may lie beyond this life. Precisely because gardening involves all five senses, the patient's experience is heightened, traveling, in Gabaldo's words, "through more sensory pathways to the brain."

THE VOCABULARY OF DESIGN

At the beginning of a new millennium it is fair to observe that what distinguishes our lives from those who have come before us is the extent to which we are separated from the cycles of nature. The fruits, vegetables, meats, and fish we buy at the supermarket arrive ready to eat or cook, the process that yielded them hidden from view. The global village of production makes it possible to eat once-seasonal fruits almost every month of the year and lets us fill our homes with flowers year-round. Even the technology that has made twentieth-century life so much kinder and gentler than it was for thousands of years has had the effect of desensitizing us to nature. As writer, horticulturist, and photographer Rick Darke comments, "We live in a time when color is so plentiful—in books, graphics, ads, movies—that our eyes are easily blinded to color and variations in the landscape. It is easy to lose touch with the sensual side of nature, the mystery in the miniature and the detail."

Working in the garden makes us pay attention to the details we miss when we're running from appointment to appointment, answering telephones and faxes, picking up the drycleaning before closing time. The spiritual food the garden provides has everything to do with the potential for life the soil beneath our feet contains—and insinuating ourselves, as gardeners and stewards, into the process

of life nature represents. Jo Carson, an herbalist who lives in California, observes, "The garden is the meeting point between the spiritual and material worlds. There is a direct relationship between the plant and the earth, and you can actually feel the life in a plant. Gardening is soothing as well as centering and grounding because it puts us in direct contact with energy and the life force."

Above: *Areas set aside for meditation need not be grand in scale; a simple bench placed in a beautiful, quiet corner will suffice.*

Deciding how to design your own sacred space is, ultimately, personal and based on your own needs. In the pages that follow we offer a guide to the different vocabularies that can be used to create a spiritual garden.

THE SPIRITUAL PALETTE: COLOR AS SYMBOL

Because color has the ability to elicit our emotions, to shape our moods, and to increase or decrease our spiritual receptivity, the effect of color in the sanctuary garden is profound. While color symbolism is a universal

A partial sampling of greens in the spiritual garden, emblems of growth. Above, left to right: Hemlock (Tsuga canadensis), hellebore (Helleborus orientalis), maidenhair fern (Adiantum pedatum).

concept, each culture on the globe has its own interpretation, often connected to rite and ritual; in ancient times the power of color to affect human feeling and perception—now recognized by science as a fact—was understood as magical in origin. Warm colors—reds, oranges, yellows—stimulate, arouse, and engage us, while cool colors—blues, violets, purples, and whites—quiet. It's important to keep in mind that, in addition to the general symbolism of tint and hue, each of us has highly personal and specific associations with any given color.

Cynthia Lawton, a former professional gardener, has had a passion for blue flowers since her childhood when, of all the plants in her mother's garden, her favorite was lobelia (*Lobelia erinus*, 'Crystal

Palace'), jewel-toned and sparkling. She plants blue flowers not simply because they are more unusual than red or yellow ones but because blue tempers the other colors around it, bringing the palette of the garden into harmony. For her blue is an emblem of the qualities she values—vision, clarity, and insight. She loves the full range of blues in the garden in both leaf and flower alike: the clear blue of the autumn plumbago (*Ceratostigma plumbaginoides*) and forget-me-not (*Myosotis* sp.), the showy drama of the delphinium (*Delphinium* sp.) and the blue-purple aster (*Stokesia laevis*) to the whispers of blue in silvery artemisia and lamb's ear (*Stachys byzantina*), among them.

We learn from working with color in the garden. The full spectrum of garden color—the subtle and not-so-subtle variations in greens, reds, yellows, whites—is, first, a lesson in the extraordinary diversity of nature and a testament to the wonder of creation. Then, too, when we take the time to look at color in the garden and put aside our habits of quick categorization and labeling, we find ourselves able to see the small variations in tone and shade in every color. And in doing so we perceive simply and purely, stripping off a layer of rational self. In the garden it becomes eminently clear that any single word we use to describe a color—"yellow" or "blue"—doesn't begin to capture what our eyes actually see, a subtle interplay of tone and texture, light and shade. Truly seeing color in the spiritual garden reminds us that our

> **Green is the fresh emblem of well-founded hopes. In blue, the spirit can wander but in green it can rest.**
>
> *Mary Webb*

range of perception is broader than our range of expression; for example, none of us, no matter how talented, can paint the rainbow as the human eye actually perceives it, comprised of more than 700 different shades. By enlarging our range of perception—our attentiveness to detail—we become more spiritually aware.

Colors form a part of spiritual traditions and cosmologies all over the world. Among many of the Native American tribes, specific colors were associated with certain deities or totemic animals, as well as the directions of the cosmos: yellow with north, blue with west, red with south, white with east; above and below, also directions, were multi-colored and black, respectively.

Among the Cherokee, colors and cardinal points came to symbolize abstractions: red, success; blue, trouble; black, death; and white, happiness. In the Christian tradition, the Trinity is often expressed in terms of color: White is the attribute of God the Father, blue of the Son, and red of the Holy Spirit. Virtues, too, take on a special hue: faith and chastity are white, hope green, and charity red.

In the spiritual garden symbolic meaning becomes part of the palette of color. Of all the colors green will, in any garden, be both the most pervasive and persuasive. Green is, first and foremost, the color of fertility and growth, youth and new beginnings, and the power of renewal; in ancient Egypt green

Each white in the garden has its own subtle shade: Here (left) a grandiflora rose 'Mount Shasta' and (right) the bark of the urn-fruited eucalyptus.

was Osiris' color, symbolic of the annual flooding of the Nile. Green was connected to water elsewhere as well: Sacred to water sprites and goddesses (the Greek Aphrodite and the Roman Venus, for example) who emerged from the waters, green was also a symbol of love. In the garden greens testify to the panoply that is spirit since no two are precisely alike. Greens encourage feelings of tranquillity and restfulness but also tend to discourage high energy or intense focus. If you intend to do spiritual work in the garden, you'll need to balance your greens with other colors.

In Western culture white is most often associated with purity and innocence, although for the ancients white was also the color of death and bleached bones. In the spiritual garden white stands for revelation, truth, and spirit; in both the pagan and Christian worlds white was an emblem of the sanctity of the priesthood. (The druid priests dressed in white, and in Middle Irish, Welsh, and Breton, a single word signifies both "white" and "blessed.") In Japan, the white lotus is the emblem of the Buddha's knowledge. The "purity" of white, though, is symbolic rather than real; when we look closely at whites in the garden we see the faint overlay of other colors—pinks, yellows, blues, greens—in

Yellow is the color of the sun, brightness, and light; in its purest form, such as the bright yellow center of the daisy, it is an emblem of happiness and hope. As writer Anne Morrow Lindbergh once observed of the bright bursts of yellow in early spring, "Forsythia is pure joy. There is not an ounce, not a glimmer of sadness or even knowledge in forsythia." In the garden yellow is also the color of cyclical nature, signaled by the changing deciduous leaves in the autumn. Depending on the depth of its tones, yellow can either

every one. Whites teach us how our perceptions are shaped by relationships: The fewer colors around it, the "whiter" a white will seem.

Red is the color of passion and fire, vivid and intense; it has signified strength and war in many cultures, and is an emblem of the masculine. But since red is the color of life-giving blood, it also has powerful associations with the feminine and special magical powers; in Hinduism red belongs to Laksmi, goddess of good fortune, fertility, beauty. Red is a stimulant, literally raising our blood pressure— which is why, in anger, we "see red." Keep in mind the full range of reds as you plant; while the bright reds of certain plants aren't conducive to contemplative spiritual activities, the

deeper, darker reds that trail off into maroon are emblematic of mystery. Use red in the spiritual palette for energy; in feng shui red is associated with the direction of south, the journey that is life, and career.

Orange has much in common with the passion of red—it, too, is associated with fire, fertility, and love—though its yellow warmth tempers its effect in the garden, and its depth of color may be comforting. Orange is also associated with fruition, harvest, and the sunset, and thus has positive personal associations for many people. As an extroverted and energetic color, orange, like red, should be used sparingly in any garden of spirit meant to encourage meditation or prayer.

A range of reds reveal themselves in the rose (opposite); the gladiolus (above left); and the nannyberry (Virburnum lentago, above right), whose leaves teach the lesson of shading.

29

energize or soothe; it renders us spiritually attentive. Used symbolically, yellow in the garden stands for illumination.

Blue is the color of the heavens and the waters, and thus a symbol of the world beyond the material; it is the color of insight, contemplation, and the infinite. In the Christian tradition it was the color of the Virgin Mary, who was depicted as wearing a blue cloak, symbolic of heaven. In many legends the Virgin Mary is credited with turning the flowers of herbs and plants blue in thanks for their help or intervention. In earlier times blue belonged to other gods and goddesses including the Egyptian Amon, the Greek Zeus, the Greek Hera, the Roman Juno, and the Hindu Vishnu, preserver of the universe and embodiment of goodness and mercy. Blue is a meditative color and encourages us to look inward with a new kind of energy; cool and detached, it is the opposite of red in the spiritual spectrum.

Purple was the color of the ancient high priests and priestesses, and thus sacral in nature; over time it became the color of royalty and thus signified high rank both

For the ancient Egyptians, blue was the color of truth; universally, it is the color of spirit. In the garden, blue takes on many shadings, from that of Greek anemone (Anemone blanda, left) to the bright clarity of sky limning the leaves and branches of trees (above) to the subtle softness of the petals of the Chilean crocus (Tecophilaea cyanocrocus, opposite).

name from the Latin word for pink. The word "pink" is a relative newcomer in English, appearing first in the seventeenth century from the common name for the dianthus, an extremely popular bedding plant that is often rose-colored. According to Louise Beebe Wilder in *The Fragrant Garden*, "pinks" were cultivated not only for their scent—the "spices in their throats"—but also for their place in the domestic pharmacopoeia where they were thought, when eaten, to comfort the heart and, when distilled, to lower fevers. In the garden of the spirit pink is a balm that quiets our jangled nerves and senses, suffusing us with peace.

Our perception of colors in the garden is affected not only by the available light but also by the interplay of colors in both the natural and artificial elements. Choosing bright colors is not the only way of giving the spiritual garden a focal point; using muted gray or brown paving stones in a garden path will emphasize the colors of the plants at its edges. On a patio or in a city backyard the earth tones of terra-cotta pots can provide a similar backdrop for emphasis. Remember to pay attention to colored

spiritually and politically. A mixture of red and blue, purple stands for balance and mediation, incorporating both the cool detachment of blue and the fire of red, the symbols of air and fire. Because purple doesn't appear often in nature except in flora (purple quartz, or amethyst, is a notable exception), most of the words describing the tones of purple are drawn from the garden: amaranthine, aubergine, heliotrope, lavender, lilac, mauve, mulberry, orchid, plum, and violet. Purple in the garden can lift our souls with positive energy.

Symbolically pink is red drained of all its bite, gentle and feminine in nature. The flower we've come to associate most intimately with love and emotion, the rose, takes its

Pinks—from the soft and delicate to the full-throated shades—calm the soul: Camellia 'Nicky Crisp' *(above);* Camellia x *'Williams Debby' (right).*

Opposite: *In this garden, blues, greens, and reds form a harmonious blanket of color, further unified by the skillful placement of the blue urn in the foreground.*

leaves and foliage as well as flowers; the color of the leaf will affect not only your perception of light in the garden but will provide the garden's basic color level long after the blooms have faded. The silvery leaves of wormwood (*Artemisia* sp.) or garden sage (*Salvia officianalis*) act as highlights, while the gold-toned greens of certain of the plantain lilies (*Hosta* 'Golden Scepter', for example) bring light into even the most shaded of areas.

As you choose plants for color, try to visualize the space in which you're working as a whole, not simply part by part; by analogy, just as body and soul are part of a single whole, color and light in the garden are aspects of one another. We would expect the high energy of red—whether in the form of a single plant or a massed planting in the garden—to dominate our field of vision, but white will function the same way if surrounded by deeper, even bolder colors. Whites reflect light, and masses of white flowers, while eye-popping in the midday sun, will give your garden a soft glow as the day winds down toward twilight. By the light of the moon white flowers will emerge from the shadows as cool, spectral presences. Consider your own needs in the spiritual garden as you plant. Using plants of similiar leaf or flower tones will give you an uninterrupted, soft flow of energy and induce

feelings of harmony, while bold contrasts—bright yellows against greens, oranges against paler plantings—will energize you and your sacred space.

ENERGY IN THE SPIRITUAL GARDEN: LIGHT, WIND, AND WATER

The Chinese understanding of energy, symbolized by the yin-yang, will be helpful as you plan your spiritual garden, whether you intend to use principles of feng shui or not. The yin-yang—the familiar icon of a circle divided by an S-curve, half black and half white with each side punctuated by a small circle of the opposite color—was once solely a feminine symbol, related to the lunar calendar. Yin and yang represent the opposite energies from which the universe and all things in it emerged. While they are opposites, they are not understood as being in opposition or as mutually exclusive; both the yin (the feminine) and the yang (the masculine) contain something of one another's nature, symbolized by the small circle of the opposite color. The yin and the yang together constitute perfect balance, precisely because the presence of one permits an understanding of the other. An overabundance of either yin or yang will yield a space that is either too dull or too charged with energy. This valuable spiritual concept is perhaps best understood in visual terms. Imagine a garden filled with plants of similar leaf shapes, heights, and colors; what is missing is all sense of texture, contrast, and light in a flood of low-energy yin. Conversely, a garden full of high-contrast colors, shapes, and heights in its plantings has too much yang, and will simply look cacophonous. (For more, see "The Feng Shui Garden," page 130.)

Balance is key to the energy level of any spiritual garden, and it's important to keep in mind that structural simplicity—fewer elements working in harmony—is not synonymous with sparseness. As Jeff Mendoza, a well-known designer of both city and country gardens, comments, "The garden is a place of reflection, whether a highly orchestrated perennial garden or a serene Japanese garden. The perennial garden reflects the abundance of nature, while the latter, when reduced to its essence, is a crystalline form of nature at its most beautiful." Seeing all the elements in the garden as contributing to the whole is one of the important spiritual lessons gardening teaches.

Natural light will affect the energy of your garden and your own energy level, and will dictate which plants

Energy made manifest in the spiritual garden. Opposite: *Pampas grass and dogwoods.* Above: *Squirreltail grass.*

you can grow easily and successfully. Areas of full sun—perfect for parts of gardens designed to awaken our senses, such as an aromatherapy garden or a saint's garden—may simply be too bright (or in summer, too hot) for an area devoted to contempla-

and sounds around you. Creating a spiritual garden teaches us, too, that the gardening terms we're used to—"full sun" or "partial shade"—are relative and, while useful as guides for planting, can't fully describe the interplay of light and dark in nat-

and amphibians—that inhabit the landscape. (It's no accident that the ancient Chinese art of energy, feng shui, literally means "wind and water.") Becoming conscious of the air's movement in the garden is a step toward full mindfulness. Wind

tion, such as a Zen or tranquillity garden. Once again, look for balance: Even though aromatic plants usually need full sun (members of the mint family, Lamaiceae, such as thyme, lemon thyme, or lavender, or heliotrope, for example), you will need an area of partial shade where you can sit and take in the scents

ural surroundings. (The "when" of full sun—in the early afternoon when the sun is strong or in the hours just before dusk—is equally important.)

Movement is an essential component of energy in the garden, supplied by wind and water, and by the creatures—insects, birds, fish,

is a symbol of the cosmic spirit, as the opening words of the book of Genesis remind us: "And the Spirit of God moved upon the face of the

Above: *The quantity and quality of light shape our understanding of the landscape. A garden in frost takes on a spectral, otherworldly aspect.*

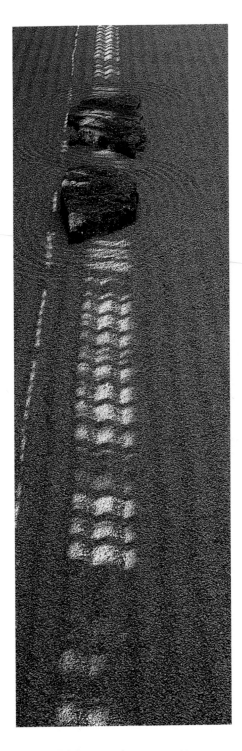

Above: *Light superimposes pattern on pattern in a raked dry Zen garden.*

waters." In the New Testament the wind brings the Apostles the Holy Spirit, while in Indian mythology wind or cosmic breath is personified by the god Vayu. Emphasize the energy of spirit in your garden by planting ornamental grasses, such as zebra grass (*Miscanthus sinensis* 'Zebrinus') or fountain grass (*Pennisetum alopecuroides*), so that air takes on the dimensions of sound and sight; the grasses, too, will enliven and bring energy to your garden in winter, long after your blooms have faded. Using artifacts in the garden—wind chimes, bells, and whirligigs, for example—also increases our awareness of the unseen energy all around us.

Energy, particularly life energy, and water are inextricably connected. The life-energy of water has been honored by humanity since at least the early Paleolithic, expressed not only in a vocabulary of graphic symbolism—spirals, whirls, and coiling forms—but also in sacred sites located near bodies of water. All over the globe the flow of water symbolizes the changeability of life: The waterfall is the emblem of continuous and ever-changing motion, the whirlpool of life's difficulties, the stream of its steady progress, and the pond of its mystery and depth. Both fluid and cohesive at once—capable of splitting off into droplets and streams and then reemerging as one—water is energy made manifest; it also symbolizes possibility. In most creation myths, including that of Genesis, the universe is begun, "hatched," or "breathed" out of or over water.

Because water is the primordial fluid, including it in our sacred space outdoors—whether in the form of a small fountain, water garden, or pond—acknowledges the rhythms and truths of the larger macrocosm. We are relaxed and soothed by the sounds of water; perhaps they are a reminder of the salty fluids in which we began our lives. A pond with its hidden depths is also a symbol of mystery, and ponds and pools are, in many cultures, associated with nymphs, sprites, and other prophetic spirits. Water, too, represents both purification and purity, which is why it plays a part in religious rituals the world over, from the Holy Water of the Christian Church to the perfumed water offerings of Tibetan Buddhism. Both dew and rainwater—pure and fresh from the heavens—were traditionally seen as divine gifts, both spiritual and material in nature.

The energy of the life force expresses itself, too, in the fauna of the spiritual garden—from the web of the uninvited (but essential) spider to the showy monarch butterfly sip-

ping from the buddleia we've planted for its pleasure and our own. Throughout the year, even in the dead of winter when the hard earth glints with frost, we can make our gardens places of sanctuary for a variety of birds—orioles, titmice, finches, chickadees, woodpeckers, wrens, and the beautiful, if fractious, bluejays—by planting with them in mind. In small ways we can, as gardeners, make ourselves a part of the life force itself.

Left: Droplets of water caught on a spider's web spun over an evergreen viola symbolize the dependence of all forms of life on water.

Above: Water endows the garden with sight, sound, energy, and life.

THE ENERGY OF SCENT: FRAGRANCE IN THE GARDEN

Scent, too, connects us to spirit in the garden. The fragrances of flowers and leaves, of freshly turned earth, the loamy smells released by a spring or summer rain, and the hint of perfume on a breeze are part of the palette of fragrance. For thousands of years, humanity has understood the power of scent to calm and soothe, invigorate and stimulate, inspire and open. Spiritual awareness has long been thought to increase through scent; our "perfume" comes from the Latin word meaning "by smoke," a reference to the burning of herbs in religious rites and activities, a practice that long predated Roman civilization and continues in churches and temples all over our contemporary world. The perfumes released by burning symbolized the presence of the deity in the sacred space, while the trails of smoke—in cultures as various as those of the Native Americans and of Buddhist Tibet—represented prayers that connected the spheres of heaven and earth. Two of the Magi's gifts to the infant Jesus—resinous gums used as incense—symbolized their recognition of the child's holiness. The use of perfumed unguents and oils for ritual and ceremonial purposes is also universal, including the chrism—a mixture of oil and balsam—used in the Catholic and Eastern Orthodox churches.

Above: *The smallest of ponds, created out of different materials, can evoke both the life force and the idea of sanctuary, and serve as a living mandala.*

Fragrance probably played a role, too, in the use of flowers as offerings to the gods and goddesses. A Sumerian seal shows worshipers carrying a garland to a temple, while in ancient Egypt, in the middle of the first millennium B.C., Ramses III created a garden to honor the god of Heliopolis, filled with "flowers from every country, sweet and fragrant." In ancient Greece garlands of fragrant flowers and leaves, particularly the myrtle, bedecked the heads of the sacrifices and those officiating the cermony, as well as the representations of the gods and goddesses. In ancient Rome, floral offerings were made to the household gods, or *lares familiares*, each morning. In contemporary times fragrant flowers are left in tribute at Catholic shrines and placed on Buddhist altars; the Hindu word for offering, *puja*, actually means "gift of fruit or flowers," and specific flowers are offered to Ganesa, Krishna, and Shiva.

The healing power of scent was also an important component of the plants included in humanity's earliest pharmacopoeia. The scent of crushed basil was thought to stimulate and lift what was then called "melancholy," and Pliny wrote that the fragrance of mint alone "recovers and refreshes our spirits." Redolent rosemary was considered among the most potent of all fragrances; its scent was believed not only to stimulate memory but also to act as a spiritual restorative. The sweet scent of oregano (its name means "joy of the mountain," *oros ganos*) was thought by the ancient Greeks to quiet the spirits of the dead as well as to invigorate those of the living.

Scent can be extraordinarily evocative—summoning past experiences, half-forgotten moments, with enormous clarity—and often begins a process of association and awakening that is different from any called up by the other senses. Fragrance in the spiritual garden can help us get in touch with our past, present, and future selves. As Alice Lounsberry wrote at the beginning of this century, "To many the perfume of flowers has more meaning than their outward beauty. In it they feel the spirit and the eternity of the flower."

Since floral scent evolved to guide and attract bees and butterflies as part of the process of fertilization,

Left: *A detail from a beautiful garden of fragrance with artemisia and heliotrope.*

CYCLICAL TIME IN THE GARDEN: THE SEASONS, THE MOON, AND THE SUN

The garden puts us back in touch with the seasons as we watch the transformation of the landscape, and permits us to see the stages of our own lives as necessary and similar in kind. In the spiritual garden the dying-off in winter holds the promise of spring, and the snow becomes a blanket protecting life below the surface. Winter allows us to see the forms and structures hidden beneath the surface, whether those are raked patterns of gravel in a Zen garden or the limned branches of a tree set against a winter sunset. In spring ancient myths of rebirth take on visible form as tender shoots give way to stem and blossom; the sudden greening of the landscape—the buds released as if by magic by warm sunlight after a spring rain—preaches homilies about moments of ripeness. The rainless drowsy air of summer leaves the earth parched and flowers wilted, a hard lesson in balance. Fall is a cool restorative and lets us take stock of ourselves; in autumn we can assess inner and outer growth alike, both in ourselves and in the garden. And the continuing cycle begins anew.

The cycles of the moon and the sun in the garden teach other impor-

fragrance in the spiritual garden is also a reminder of the web of relationship. As Rosemary Verey wrote in *The Scented Garden*, "Were it not for this symbiotic relationship, flowers might have evolved without scent." It is no exaggeration to reflect that, had evolution chosen another path, the world in which humans live would be a place poorer in spirit.

Above: *In this spiritual garden, a path lined by lavender promises to awaken all of the senses.*

Above right: *The seasonal renewal of spirit is captured in both the gentle riot of color and scent of the magnolia's blooms.*

Finally, fragrance in the spiritual garden teaches us about the amazing diversity of flora, for no two fragrances are precisely the same. On a more contemplative note, fragrance is a lesson in the fleeting nature of beauty—which is why scented flowers have traditionally been a part of burial ceremonies. In the words of the Psalms, "As for a man, his days are as grass: as a flower of the field, so he flourisheth. For the wind passeth over it, and it is gone; and the place thereof shall know it no more." (For more on fragrance, see "The Aromatherapy Garden," page 122.)

For everything
there is a season,
and a time for every
purpose under
the heaven:
a time to be born,
and a time to die;
a time to plant,
and a time to pluck up
that which is planted.

Ecclesiastes

Each season has a splendor all its own.

Opposite: *The soft glow of a crabapple in spring, at Shoyoan Teien, the Japanese Garden at Wesleyan University.*

Top right: *The brilliance of a perennial border in summer.*

Middle right: *A Japanese maple set against a white birch in autumn.*

Bottom right: *An herb garden, crystalline in winter frost.*

In the spiritual garden, the sun as the emblem of growth and life takes on a new reality; we watch the seedling flourish in the light, and the flower arc its stem toward it. As the sun rises in the sky from spring to mid-summer, so does the garden grow and flourish. The shortening of the days and the lowered sun, conversely, signal a seasonal end. The solar symbolism of illumination and manifestation takes on a literal aspect when the first rays of light bring morning to the darkened forms of the garden and make them literally manifest. The ever-changing tones of light, from sunrise to sunset, teach another lesson about cyclical time, and the ever-changing nature of the world we live in.

Rick Darke and his wife, Melinda Zoehrer, a horticulturist, have designed their garden to capture patterns of light emanating from the cycles of the sun and the moon. Darke feels strongly, as did Emerson and the Transcendentalists who have influenced him, that the spiritual lessons of nature have to be part of "your necessary journey," not separate from daily life but wholly integrated into it. To that end, the boundaries between interior and exterior space in his home and garden have been deliberately blurred by the installation of glass walls in those rooms—the bedroom, the bathroom, the living and eating areas—where life actually takes place. In Darke's own words, "the garden can a be a tool to immerse yourself if the garden is the place where you go about the business of life." Even when he and Melinda are inside, they are also in the garden. Different aspects of the garden's design work to highlight the cycles of light. A border of mountain silverbells (*Halesia tetraptera*), two-winged silverbells (*Halesia diptera* var. *magniflora*) and dwarf fothergillas (*Fothergilla gardenii*) has been planted on an axis with the rising sun and moon so that it is bathed in all kinds of seasonal light. In addition Rick and Melinda have planted ornamental grasses so that they are backlit by the sun. Among the plants Darke recommends for catching and

tant lessons of spirit. The recurring drama of the night sky—the growth, death, and then apparent rebirth of the shining moon—puts us back in touch with mysteries of the past. In ancient times, humanity knew the moon as the creator of the tides and as she who made the sap rise; moonlight was thought to be the force that energized the sprouting seed, and thus planting took place during moontimes, not during the day. Early peoples thought, too, that because moisture swelled up out of the earth during the waxing moon, it was the best time to sow leafy plants that grew above the ground; conversely the time of the waning moon was right for planting tubers, which grow below the surface, and trees and shrubs which need strong roots.

reflecting light in the garden are prairie dock (*Silphium terebinthinaceum*), switch grass (*Panicum virgatum*), and 'Sioux Blue' Indian grass (*Sorghastrum nutans* 'Sioux Blue'). Two sculptures in their garden—one natural in origin, the other man-made—accentuate the solar and lunar cyles. Rough-hewn, salvaged cedar posts frame the rising sun and moon in every season, while a sculpture of glass panes—recycled from the conservatory at Longwood Gardens where Darke was the curator of plants—reflect sun rays and moonbeams throughout the year.

Coming to terms with time in the garden must, finally, be what it's like to catch a glimpse of eternity: an endless, ever-circling sweep of motion pulling us from sunrise to sunset, again and again.

CREATING A SYMBOLIC LANDSCAPE: STONE, WOOD, PATHS, AND SACRED GEOMETRY

In the spiritual garden, design involves more than aesthetics. Developing a garden landscape that can evoke a sense of awe and articulate the soul requires that we pay attention to pattern and symbol. We look to elements of design not simply to beautify but to increase our awareness of our surroundings and to open up the nuances and meanings inherent in the natural world. Whether we choose to work with a symbolic system dictated by tradition—such as a feng shui, Zen, or labyrinth garden—or

Observing time in the garden teaches an important lesson of spirit and permits us to get in touch with the larger cycles of nature.

Opposite top: *The rising sun captured in Rick Darke and Melinda Zoehrer's garden.*

Opposite bottom: *The full moon framed between the cedar posts.*

Right: *A sundial in a beautiful sanctuary not only acts as a focal point but increases our awareness of time. Here, the sundial is framed by salvia and African daisy.*

45

decide to design our gardens based on a combination of personal and traditional associations is less important than our commitment to creating a sanctuary that lets us journey out of the everyday jangle of things to meaningful thought.

Spiritual garden design makes us look at the elements in our garden anew, both those natural to the landscape and those we've chosen for it. Objects made of natural materials—stone and wood—ground us in the garden. The presence of stone in the sanctuary garden—whether that of a rough-hewn rock dug out of the earth, a bench or paving stone, or the deliberate arrangement of moss-covered and weathered stones in the Zen garden—symbolizes the eternal, permanent, and unchanging. In cultures all over the world, stone was understood as an abode of the gods and the supernatural; to peoples as various as the Native Americans, the ancient Greeks, and the Mesopotamians, rocks were the offspring of the Earth Mother. In the spiritual garden, stone is a visual emblem

unchanging values and stability, including fairness, integrity, and justice, as some of our expressions remind us ("a square meal," "fair and square," and the like); square elements in the spiritual garden encourage us to make stable connections, to focus on the here and now, not the ephemeral. Like the square the rectangle stands for permanence and is essentially static and earthbound. Finally, the triangle is a powerful and ancient emblem of the feminine, associated with life, procreation, and water. In the Pythagorean system the triangle, the simplest of geometric figures, symbolized wisdom.

There are many different ways of incorporating the circle, the square, or the triangle, alone or in combination, into the design of your sanctuary. Creating a knot garden of herbs—best situated where it can be seen from above—is one way of using sacred geometry to create a place of quiet and stasis. While the knot garden is usually identified with England, where the form flourished in the sixteenth and seventeenth centuries, its

earliest appearance was in ancient Sumer some 5,000 years ago; its components were also a part of the walled gardens of Persia. The knot is an ancient symbol of continuity in cultures all over the world; interwoven, seemingly without beginning or end, like the circle the

The smallest of details leads the eye into the heart of the garden. Opposite left: A carefully laid pathway of stones.

Opposite far left: *The lines of a stone lantern are set against the grace of the irises nearby.*

Above: *The combination of the seasonal and the permanent, symbolized by the azaleas in flower and a carefully placed rock, is visual shorthand for the nature of the universe in the Japanese garden.*

Left: *A beautiful fountain, filled with smooth pebbles, provides the focal point for this sanctuary.*

most important, closely related to the spiral, which symbolizes energy or the life force. Because it echoes the shapes of the heavenly bodies—the sun, the moon, and, as humanity later would discover, the earth itself—the circle has always stood for the cosmic order and the spirit that animates the cosmos. For Native Americans the circle of the cosmos (punctuated by the six directions) provided the sacred model for all human activities. All of life was given ritual meaning by incorporating the circle into everyday detail—from the circular arrangement of dwellings, to eating, meeting, and dancing in circles, to artifacts such as the medicine wheel. As an image of eternity—often pictured as a snake with its tail in its mouth—the circle also symbolized the cyclical nature of life, the wheel that is ever turning. Immutable, the circle in the Christian tradition, along with the ring, becomes a monogram for God, "who was in the beginning, is now, and ever shall be, without end." The center of the circle, too, suggests a cosmic and spiritual focal point, while the enclosure the circle provides is an image of protection. It's no wonder that the circle is the template for holy places and rites, particularly those pertaining to fertility. Circular forms make us keenly aware of the process of unfolding—of revelation in time—which is a part of the overall pattern of life; the unfolding spiral has its basis in nature. The daisy and other members of the Asteraceae family begin as a green circular knob that opens to reveal a bright yellow center surrounded by the white, raylike petals that give the flower its common name ("the day's eye"); at the end of the flowering cycle the petals

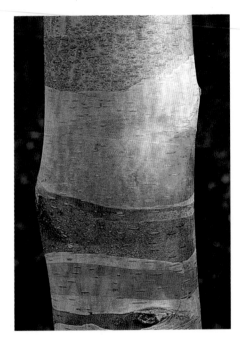

drop off, returning the flower to the circular form once more. The coils of the cinnamon fern (*Osmunda cinnamomea*) embody the energy inherent in the spiral: out of the tight circle of the fiddlehead comes the extraordinary burst of the frond. The round but spiky flowerheads of the globe thistle (*Echinops*) teach us

that, in nature, the circle and the sphere can take on a variety of textures. The circular form of many seedpods is a reminder, too, that the circle is the shape of new beginnings. Seeing the round seedpod of the plane tree or sycamore (*Platanus* sp.), we understand why the Egyptian goddess Hathor took on the form of the sycamore when she fed the souls of the dead.

Nature speaks in symbols and in signs.

John Greenleaf Whittier

Other geometric shapes, not necessarily found in the flora of the garden, can be used in conjunction with the circle or alone to create sacred space outdoors, and should be kept in mind as you create beds, walkways, and even seating areas. The square, with its four equal sides, is the most grounded of geometric figures; it is usually a symbol of earth—solid, permanent, unmoving—while the fluid circle is the emblem of heaven. The square is associated with unchanging values and stability, including fairness, integrity, and justice, as some of our expressions remind us ("a square meal," "fair and square," and the like); square elements in the spiritual garden encourage us to

make stable connections, to focus on the here and now, not the ephemeral. Like the square the rectangle stands for permanence and is essentially static and earthbound. Finally, the triangle is a powerful and ancient emblem of the feminine, associated with life, procreation, and water. In the Pythagorean system the triangle, the simplest of geometric figures, symbolized wisdom.

Opposite: *Wood, considered the primordial matter in many cultures, takes on even more meaning when fashioned into a gate, symbol of the passage from one plane of existence to another.*

Above left and above: *The rich texture of aged birch wood makes it clear why wood was an emblem of the immortal spirit.*

Above, opposite left, opposite right: *The carved spiral in a stone pathway; the web of a garden spider; the raked pattern of gravel. Because it has no beginning and no end, the circle also symbolizes eternity, equality, unity, and relation. In the garden, the circle—the emblem of the cosmic order—takes on many forms, some natural, others crafted.*

There are many different ways of incorporating the circle, the square, or the triangle, alone or in combination, into the design of your sanctuary. Creating a knot garden of herbs—best situated where it can be seen from above—is one way of using sacred geometry to create a place of quiet and stasis. While the knot garden is usually identified with England, where the form flourished in the sixteenth and seventeenth centuries, its earliest appearance was in ancient Sumer some 5,000 years ago; its components were also a part of the walled gardens of Persia. The knot is an ancient symbol of continuity in cultures all over the world; interwoven, seemingly without beginning or end, like the circle the knot symbolizes infinity. In Buddhism the endless knot is one of the eight sacred symbols. In ancient Egypt, the knot was an emblem of life; elsewhere it symbolizes bonds and partnership—which is why, when we marry, we "tie the knot." Knots also have magical overtones as talismans of protection; it's likely that the enclosure of the knot garden conferred protection on its owners from malign influences. As a carefully designed symbolic landscape, the knot garden could stand for any number of things, depending on the patterns of its design and the symbolism of the plants within it. Some knot gardens were spiritual in nature—signifying, variously, the commitment of partnership, the journey of life, or the specifically Christian pilgrimage—while others were secular in content.

Remember that the spiritual exercise of the knot garden is one of discipline; this garden requires very specific maintenance—forethought as to the hardiness of the plants in your area, as well as constant pruning, weeding, and tending. Among the plants traditionally used to create the knot's outlines are dark green wall germander (*Teucrium chamaedrys*), barberry (*Berberis*), and varieties of boxwood (*Buxus* sp.); the interior of the knot can be planted with all manner of herbs, including varieties of

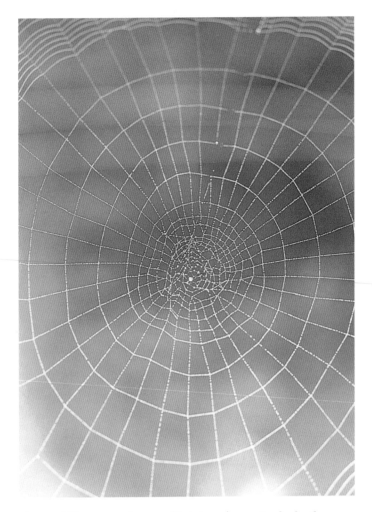

thyme (*Thymus* sp.), sage (*Salvia* sp.), particularly the compact purple sage *S. purpurea* and the green and gold *S. officinalis* 'Icterina', rosemary (*Rosmarinus officinalis*), different lavenders (*Lavandula angustifolia*) and hyssop (*Hyssopus officinalis*). As you choose the plants for your knot garden, keep in mind that you'll want them to grow to—or be pruned back to—compatible heights; you can also choose plants for color, contrast, symbolic meaning, or even their medicinal use.

Symbolic shapes can also be used to design walkways, paths of meditation, even labyrinths. The biblical garden planted and designed by Donna Hopper and Brenda Corey at St. Paul's, an Episcopal church in

Connecticut, was conceived as a tool of evangelism or, as Brenda puts it, "a visible prayer." All of the plants within it were chosen either because they are mentioned in the Bible or because they are associated with the Virgin Mary and other saints in legend. Since the garden fronts a busy and heavily trafficked street, it functions as a literal reinforcement of the spirit of church community and an invitation to the public, rather than as a place of meditation. The garden is shaped in the form of a Celtic cross, with a circle at its very center; the form of the cross naturally divides into quadrants, while the circle gives the garden a focal point in which a fig tree dominates. The success of this spiritual garden has

inspired the congregation to plan an addition, this one in the shape of a bishop's mitre.

Working in a completely different spiritual tradition, Alex Champion, a builder of mazes and labyrinths on the West Coast, author of *Earth Mazes*, and a Ph.D. in biochemistry, uses many different patterns for his work—the six-pointed star, double spirals, figure eights, meanders, and traditional three- and four-ringed Cretan labyrinthine designs, among others. Alex reminds us that when the symbolic geometric form is used as the tem-

Above: *Photographer John Glover's garden is designed in the shape of a mandala and is oriented to the four directions. At its center, visible from the meditation bench, is a pond, home to frogs and newts. The surrounding beds of thyme as well as other herbs attract many kinds of wildlife, particularly bees and butterflies.*

Opposite: *An open gate and a partly visible path invite us on a journey of discovery.*

plate either for a walkway or a labyrinth, "you're actually inside the symbol and the energy field it creates." (For more on the labyrinth and its use as a spiritual tool, see page 156.)

Paths and pathways, along with other garden design elements with a strong symbolic basis, take on a particular importance in the spiritual garden. Paths stand for the spiritual course of life, the journey toward self-realization, and pilgrimage; walking along a path—even a short one—is a useful spiritual tool for grounding as well as meditation. In her book *Walking a Sacred Path*, the Reverend Dr. Lauren Artress writes, "To walk a sacred path is to discover our inner sacred space: that core of feeling that is waiting to have life breathed into it through symbols, archetypal forms like the labryinth, rituals, stories, and myths." Steps and stairs—versions of the ladder—also have symbolic meaning in the spiritual tradition, and can be used to great effect in the garden. Since ancient times, steps have been emblems of both the ascent of the soul and the link between earth and heaven; generally they stand for the acquisition of spiritual knowledge and the process of spiritual transformation. (In ancient Egypt the souls of the dead were pictured ascending nine steps to the throne of Osiris.) In the spiritual garden steps—even those that mark just a slight change in grade—offer a changing perspective on the landscape; stairs also encourage us to pause, slow down, and become aware of slight but meaningful variations in the garden. Rick Darke, writer, photographer, and horticulturist, uses the analogy of experiencing the "architecture of the winter woods." As he puts it, "We really see the complexity of the landscape when we look up at the canopy of the forest, with its branches in silhouette. Move forward one foot, look again, and thousands of angles have changed." The landing of steps can be used as seating or, if broad enough, home to a bench for contemplation. Steps need not be rectangular in

shape; round pavers, made of prepoured concrete, can suggest the flow of water or symbolize continuity and relationship. Equally, a terraced garden can suggest different levels of spiritual awakening.

CREATING A SANCTUARY: GATES, DOORS, AND TRANSITIONS

Sacred space outdoors is often deliberately set apart from the distractions of daily life—the ring of telephones and faxes, the errands to be run, and all manner of everyday demands—to permit us to focus on our spiritual work. Gates and doorways, as well as fences and dividers, emphasize the spiritual garden as a site of sanctuary and safety. Traditionally, gates symbolize places of passage, separating one state or reality from another; in the Judeo-Christian tradition, doors were a symbol of revelation and God's manifestation. Symbolically, Jesus Christ is the doorway to redemption, as is made clear in the Book of John: "I am the door: by me, if any man enter in, he shall be saved." All over the world, doors to sacred places—whether those of a Buddhist temple or a church—acknowledge the transition between the realm of the profane and the realm of the sacred. For the same reason thresholds—areas symbolic of transition and passage—were considered sacred from Greek and Roman times forward.

   The areas of the home that serve as places of transition from the interior of the house to the spiritual

Opposite left and right: *Stepping stones, traditionally used in Zen stroll and tea gardens, or irregularly placed flagstones slow the pace of the observer as an aid to meditation and absorption in the landscape.*

Right: *The inner sanctum of a spiritual garden is glimpsed through a beautifully wrought gateway, visually preparing the visitor for the transition into sacred space.*

garden—the doors and door frames, windows, porches, or mud rooms—and back function as part of the garden itself. Karen Lukas, an artist who specializes in the creation of healing and sacred spaces, reminds us that a transitional area is "a place where we shed something and prepare to take on something else." Most importantly, she

tation room she designed as the transition into Stephen Huyler's spiritual garden in Maine was envisioned as an extension of the garden, facilitating the journey from inside to outside and back. Karen used more than 300 pigments in the space, the colors of the natural world—reds to oranges to yellows to blues to purples to peach and then back to reds—blending into one another with extraordinary subtlety and depth. Written on the walls beneath the layers of paint—invisible to the eye, but present nonetheless—are words of inspiration drawn from poems and other writings compiled by Huyler, his friends, and mentors. The ceiling of the room is painted as sky, and niches in the walls hold spiritual statuary. The glass doors giving out onto the garden are covered in gold leaf, signaling the transition from one plane to another.

says, it's a "place of shifting scales—of changes in size, color, light or feeling—and if a space has a very strong identity, it is not functioning as transitional space even if it is physically a passageway."

For one of her clients, she painted a second-story screened-in porch, used for teaching yoga classes, in a range of greens, bringing the serenity of the treetops outside and the garden below into the space itself. The interior medi-

Above left: *Landscape designer Chris Jacobson's city garden is a "safe zone of green," a place of respite experienced from inside the house as well as outside.*

Above right: *Steps create different levels of experience in the journey through this spiritual garden.*

Right: *Stephen Huyler's meditation room and the gilded doors that give way to his garden sanctuary.*

Remember that the design of these areas of transition doesn't need to be costly or even elaborate. Painting the back door that leads to the garden in soft and soothing shades may give you just enough room to take a deep, even breath before you move toward awakening your soul outside.

THE SPIRITUAL LANGUAGE OF PLANTS AND TREES

When most of us think about the "language of flowers," what is most likely to come to mind is the Victorian vocabulary of sentiment: By sending a bouquet or a tussie-mussie to a lady, a gentleman might, with the right combination of flowers, communicate his heart's desire

without ever saying a word. A red rose assured the recipient of fidelity and love, while a white one signified a pure love; a yellow rose referred to the sender's jealousy. The iris signaled rejection, while the presence of a forget-me-not was self-explanatory. Yet this somewhat cloying nineteenth-century convention—still familiar through reproductions of antique books and cards—grows out of a much older and more serious sacral tradition, which can be made a part of a contemporary spiritual garden. Choosing what we plant for meaning and the creation of a symbolic landscape can be an essential component of spiritual gardening.

The importance of flowers, plants, and trees to humanity's spiritual life is preserved for us in ancient art and artifact. Statuary and funerary objects dating from the sixth millennium B.C. bear patterns identified as those of sprouting seeds, which were emblems of rebirth and symbolic of a belief in an afterlife. Images from Minoan civilization, which flourished between 3000 and 1400 B.C., make it clear that groves of trees—chestnut, oak, cypress, palm,

Left: *The three-petalled iris is an emblem of the Trinity.*

Right: *A beautifully crafted bowl becomes a miniature garden of spirit, complete with a water lily, indicative of the sacred.*

and cedar—were sacred ritual sites; poppies, later sacred to Hera in ancient Greece, crown figurines of Minoan earth goddesses as emblems of fecundity. In ancient Egypt, the lotus not only inspired ornamental patterns but also was associated with fertility, resurrection, and the sun, the latter perhaps because of its ray-like petals and habit of opening in the morning, closing at night, and then reopening the following dawn. (The sun was thought to sleep nestled in its petals.) Sacred to Horus, god of the sun, and to Osiris, god of growth and resurrection, the flower we call the Egyptian lotus was actually a water lily: the white lotus (*Nymphaea lotus*) and the fragrant blue lotus (*N. caerulea*). A funerary mural from the fifteenth century B.C.

now preserved in the Metropolitan Museum of Art in New York City shows not only a garden but also a pool of water in which the boat carrying the coffin of the deceased is moored; stylized lotuses, some budding, some blooming, emerge from the water around the boat, symbolizing rebirth. The ancient association of the lotus with resurrection may be partly based in observation because of the long viability of its seed; remarkably enough, a 2,000-year-old lotus seed was successfully germinated by a horticulturist at the National Arboretum several years ago!

The depth and subtlety of the spiritual language of flowers is revealed in the complexity of the symbolism of the lotus, and its significance in Hinduism and Buddhism.

Some of the lotus's meaning evolved out of its physical characteristics: Rooted in the mud yet growing up through water toward the sky, it symbolized the mind opening up to revelation. Because it appears to float on the waters without attachment, it is an emblem of the spirit unsullied by ignorance, reaching toward enlightenment or nirvana. Thus the Buddha is depicted standing or sitting on a lotus, sometimes with a lotus in his hand. The lotus is also a symbol of the womb as well as creation; in Hinduism the lotus grew from the navel of Vishnu as he gave birth to Brahma, making it an emblem of both cre-

Above left: *Two flowers symbolic of seasonal and spiritual renewal, crocus* (Crocus tomasinianus) *and snowdrop* (Galanthus sp.), *blanket the ground of Painswick Abbey.*

Above: *The snowdrop symbolized consolation and hope, and was thus an emblem of the Virgin Mary and the feast of her Purification on February 2, sometimes called Candlemas.*

ation and spiritual transformation. The combination of the stem (the masculine) and the blossom (the female) makes the lotus a symbol of spiritual unity; in Tibetan Buddhism the mantra *om mani padme hum* means "So be it, Jewel in the Lotus, Amen."

In the Western tradition, while many plants have spiritual meaning, none is as important as the rose, particularly the red rose. The flower's association with romantic love actually derives from a spiritual tradition that flourished in Greek and Roman cultures. The rose was sacred to the goddess of love, the Greek Aphrodite and the Roman Venus, and an emblem of the story of Adonis, one of the many ancient myths of the dying-off and the return of vegetation in the seasonal cycle. (In fact, the name Adonis comes from the Semitic word for "lord," and originally referred to the Babylonian god Tammuz, consort of the earth goddess Ishtar.) When Adonis, Aphrodite's paramour, was killed while boar hunting, the

goddess of love was inconsolable. To assuage her grief the gods permitted Adonis to return from the land of the dead for six months each spring; his reunion with Aphrodite signaled the rebirth and flowering of the natural world. In different variations of the myth, the red color of the rose either symbolized Adonis's blood, shed to bring eternal life back to earth, or Aphrodite's, a symbol of transcendent

Above left: *The sunflower was worshiped by the Incas as an emblem of the sun; both the flower and sacred images of it rendered in gold were used in ceremony and rite.*

Above right: *In China, the peony symbolizes the yang principle and is one of the flowers representing the four seasons.*

love. In ancient Greece women in mourning planted "gardens of Adonis"—pots filled with fast-growing seeds such as fennel and parsley—in courtyard gardens to honor the god's and spring's return.

In later Christian tradition, the red rose remained a potent symbol, still closely connected to blood and

Left: *The exquisite lotus rising on its slender stem toward the sun symbolizes spiritual fulfillment.*

Above: *In China, the lotus is an emblem of time past, present, and future since the plant manifests bud, flower, and seed at once. In India, it symbolizes the feminine and the generative power of the womb. A figure of a wide-hipped fertility goddess, unearthed in the Indus Valley and dating from as early as the third millenium, wears a lotus blossom in her hair.*

resurrection; the rose belongs to Jesus Christ as a symbol of both his love for humanity and his suffering on the Cross. The multipetaled rose was also a mystical emblem of the heart and the wheel of life which is the center of the cosmos. This symbolism would, in the Western tradition, give us the rose windows of the Gothic cathedral. The thornless white rose, on the other hand, belonged to the Virgin Mary, an emblem of her purity. Although the symbolism of the rose is preeminent in honoring the Virgin Mary, many other flowers are also associated with her. (For more, see "The Saint's Garden," page 150.)

Choosing plants and trees according to their meaning is another way of enriching and articulating the spiritual nature of the immediate landscape, as well as letting the garden "tell" a sacred story, as it did for thousands of years in many traditions. The iris in all of its varieties conjures up the Greek goddess of the rainbow of the same name; like the rainbow the iris symbolizes a bridge between heaven and earth, which is why, in the Christian tradition, the flower belonged to the Virgin Mary as mediator. Other flowers, such as heliotrope, chrysanthemum, and sunflower, are associated with the light and the life-giving sun. The fragrant heliotrope, as its name indicates, signifies the daily course of the sun and its light, which the flower was thought to follow; in the Christian tradition, it was associated with the Virgin Mary and other saints. In the Orient, the emblem of the sun was the chrysanthemum, because of its raylike petals; it symbolized the joining of heaven and earth, fullness and completeness, as well as immortality. The sunflower, native to the American continent, was sacred to many of its native peoples, including the Incas who revered it as a representation of the sun god.

Vines, particularly the grape vine, have important symbolic mean-

Above left: *The chrysanthemum* (**Chrysanthemum maximum**) *is a fitting solar symbol, connected to warmth and fertility.*

Above center: *The rose, here* **Rosa 'Ruby Wedding'**, *the queen of spiritual flowers in the West.*

Above: *The flowering vine is an emblem of the Tree of Life, here combined with sweet scent in the poet's jessamine* (**Jasminum officinalis**).

ing in both the pagan and Judeo-Christian traditions, and are a welcome addition to many gardens of spirit. In general terms the vine is an emblem of fecundity and spiritual life, as well as regeneration (it was sacred to

Above: *The yew* (Taxus baccata) *was associated with immortality and resilience and was often planted in graveyards and other sacred places, as this ancient example at Waverly Abbey attests.*

both Isis and Osiris in ancient Egypt); in the Old Testament, the vine is both the gift of life and the spiritual treasure God offers to humanity to make life worth living. In the New Testament the vine is a symbol of Christ. Among the vines you may want to plant are those which bear aromatic flowers such as trumpet vine (*Campsis* sp.), honeysuckle (*Lonicera* sp.), and jasmine (*Jasminum* sp.).

Trees, in or around the spiritual garden, are an important part of the symbolic landscape. In most culture, the tree is an emblem of the three realms: Its roots reach deep into the netherworld, its trunk grows out of the earth, and its branches reach into the sky or the heavens. The Tree of Life is a metaphor for all of creation, while the birds that nest in its branches represent the soul or spirit. The fruit-bearing tree is also a symbol of the fecund earth mother and thus the emblem of goddesses such as the Egyptian Hathor and the Greek Artemis; in patriarchal religions it's a symbol of God's bounty. Trees are also associated with spiritual vision (Buddha, for example, attained enlightenment under the bodhi, or fig tree), while both individual trees and groves were sites of ancient ritual and divination. Many of the Native American peoples considered the tree so sacred in nature that rituals of thanks and celebration were performed first if a living tree needed to be felled. Among the many individual trees with specific sacral histories are oak, cypress, hawthorn, hazel, ash, cedar, fig, myrtle, pine, spruce, willow, sycamore, yew, and poplar. (For more on their specific meanings, see the Index and "The Gaia Garden," page 112, "The Biblical Garden," page 144, and "The Celtic Garden," page 138.)

Working with the symbolism of plants not only enlarges our undestanding of the landscape as meaningful in all of its details but also permits us to share the visions of our ancestors, who saw the signature of the divine in all that surrounded them.

THE WEB OF LIFE: COMPANION PLANTING

The intricate relationships that reveal themselves in the garden teach us about the myriad connections in our spiritual and emotional lives, and show that interdependency is an essential component of life. The template that nature provides is not that of the hermit but that of community, and the mutually beneficial relationships among plants both in the wild and in the garden provide us with a model for seeing our lives and all of our relationships—both the intimate and the casual—in a spiritual context. In the wild, plants grow in close proximity and thrive because one plant offers another precisely the living conditions it needs; thus a deep-rooted plant provides its shallow-rooted companion the broken-up soil it requires to flourish while the shade cast by a tall plant filters the sunlight for another. In other cases, companions can either attract pollinators for their neighbors or repel noxious insects, while tap-rooted plants such as dandelions bring up the necessary minerals for their companions' growth. Writer, teacher, and herbalist Robin Rose Bennett points out that in nature companions that complement each other in their healing properties—such as burdock and dandelion, both of which can be helpful in restoring digestion—often grow together.

In cultivated space, companion planting, as it has come to be known, is probably an ancient technique. The Native Americans practiced it by planting corn, squash, and beans together in a mound of earth; the Iroquois called the ensemble "The Three Sisters," or "Daughters of Mother Earth." When in time the corn grew straight, it provided a perch for the beans, while the squash trailed

Right: *In forest and garden alike, the patterns of growth and decay are one, the death of one plant yielding to the life of another. Pictured here, on the forest floor, fungi emerge, spectre-like, from decaying wood.*

down over the mound, crowding out the weeds in its path. An offering of fish was left within the mound for the planted kernel of corn, whose honorifics were "She Who Sustains Us," "Our Mother," and "Our Life," for the central role the grain played in Native American culture. Science has confirmed why this ancient form of spiritual gardening works: The corn and the squash use the nitrogen provided by the beans, while the fish replaces the nutrients leached from the soil by the plants. The mound, precursor of the raised bed, supplied drainage. While some of the tenets of companion planting have been scientifically validated, others have their basis in the testimony of many thousands of gardeners and in folklore.

For the spiritual garden, companion planting can be a tool of awareness, communicating an important lesson about the pattern of "companionship." In the plant world, as in our own, there are sympathies and antipathies. The French marigold (*Tagetes patula*), for

Sunflowers (*Helianthus annuus*), meanwhile, produce a substance that inhibits the growth of nitrogen-fixing bacteria in the soil, and their seed hulls contain a substance that can prevent other flowers from germinating in seasons to come. In the herb garden the antipathy between basil (*Ocimum basilicum*) and rue (*Ruta graveolens*) has been noted since early in the seventeenth century; judging by the number of plants that don't thrive in rue's company, it's best to plant it on its own. (Note, too, that touching or brushing up against rue can cause a rash in some people; plant it away from pathways.) By the same token the base of every tree is not necessarily a place of sanctuary, nor is every "companionship" a match made in heaven; plants, like people, have their own defense mechanisms for survival. Alleopathic plants, as they are called, ensure their own survival by releasing inhibiting substances into the soil and air; they are hermits by definition and make poor companions. The most famous example, perhaps, is the black walnut tree (*Juglans nigra*), which has been known to be hostile to other plants—rhododenrons, blackberries, apple trees, among them—since 50 A.D. Don't plant beneath a maple tree (*Acer* sp.) both because of its shallow root system and its root secretion of a growth-inhibiting substance; the sycamore (*Platanus occidentalis*) also inhibits the growth of other herbaceous species, while its fallen leaves reduce seed germination.

Companion planting in the spiritual garden is yet another way of understanding the extraordinary complexity and variety of relationships in the natural world. While, historically, the cultivated garden has been a controlled monoculture, with little variety in plantings,

Above left: *In the spiritual garden, companion planting— here lettuce and cabbage with chives and fennel—is not simply useful but teaches an important lesson.*

Opposite: *A bee lights on a pincushion flower* (Scabiosa atropurpurea).

example, discourages nematodes as a result of a chemical exuded by its roots and is thus a great companion for potatoes as well as other flowers, including dahlias, calendulas, and chrysanthemums. Members of the *Allium*, or garlic, family will keep aphids off your roses, as will spearmint (*Mentha spicata*) and coriander (*Coriandrum sativum*). Dandelions (*Taraxacum officinale*) will increase the aroma of herbs and help flowers to grow and fruits to ripen more quickly, but can also stunt their growth.

nature's model is one of diversity and interrelationship, requiring us, as gardeners, to see each plant both individually and as part of the community. Sometimes, as Robert Frost wrote, "good fences make good neighbors"; certain plants, like people, aren't suited for the life of community unless they are specially and carefully handled. As you plan your spiritual garden take steps to understand the nature and habits of your plants; some, such as bee-balm (*Monarda* sp.), ribbon-grass (*Phalaris* sp.), cornflower (*Centaurea cyanus*), black-eyed Susan (*Rudbeckia* sp.), loosestrife (*Lysimachia* sp.), and bamboo, will, under the right circumstances, become invasive and destroy the community around them.

ALL CREATURES GREAT AND SMALL: MESSENGERS OF SPIRIT

Even the smallest of garden plots reveals the awesome and intricate plan behind all creation and gives us a fuller understanding of why, for thousands of years, humanity viewed the fauna of the garden as part of a larger pattern of divine intention. In the spiritual garden we step back from the cold clarity of scientific explanation and let ourselves appreciate the miracle and mystery of nature's workings. We wonder at the reciprocal adaptations which make it possible for a bee to light on a flower: the bee's enlarged hind feet and pollen baskets of stiff hairs, made to trap and transport pollen, and the design of his lip, perfect for sucking nectar; the bait of the flower's aroma and color, and, sometimes, the open invitation of its blossom. For the ancients, while the hard-working bee was a symbol of the material, he was also the creator of honey, a divine essence fit for offerings to the gods. (Honey is completely of nature, pure in spirit, and needs no preparation to be eaten.) The bee thus was also an emblem of the spirit and the soul, and associated with the divine from the time of the ancient Egyptians, who thought it was born of the tears of the sun god, Ra, through the Christian era where it symbolized the Word and God's gifts. The Native Americans, particularly the Hopi, used honey in their medicine ceremonies. Now our precise knowledge of the bee's contribution to the life of the garden only increases our admiration for him. Pollination in the garden—the process by which pollen is transferred to the stigma of a flower so that seeds can be produced—is part of an intricate pattern of divine collusion which involves not only bees but also birds, snails, bats, crawling and hopping insects, gusts of wind, and even raindrops.

The details of the sanctuary garden initiate us into beauty and mystery. We marvel at the work of the diligent if homely earthworm, simply but perfectly constructed to swallow and then excrete organic material into the soil. It's no wonder that these extraordinarily helpful creatures who aerate and mix the earth's surface symbolize the passage from death to life, for they facilitate plant growth. And then there are the benefi-

cial insects, those whose goals meet ours in the garden. (When using a word like "beneficial," however, keep in mind, as William Longgood wisely put it, that "We do not know how extensive or interrelated is the interlocking web of life or the penalty of disrupting it." Even those that don't share our immediate goals may be there for a reason.) The ladybug, beloved of children and gardeners alike, looks sweet but not to an aphid's eyes; she feeds on destructive, plant-eating insects at the prodigious rate of 40 or so an hour. It's no wonder that this member of the beetle family was considered sacred to the Virgin Mary (hence the name "Our Lady's Bug") who, legend has it, dispatched the ladybug to the aid of pious thir-

teenth-century French farmers praying for her intervention when their crops were beset by aphids.

And then, too, there are the garden's denizens who seem to be spirit incarnate. The dragonfly that hovers above a pool or pond is surely the Nureyev of the insect world; ethereal, shimmering, iridescence in motion. It's easy to see why the dragonfly was once a symbol of the soul. The butterfly, whether the flashy monarch or the shy cabbage white, is nothing less than a small miracle of transformation; its amazing life cycle—from egg to caterpillar to chrysalis to butterfly—made it, in ancient times and now, a fitting emblem of the imperishable soul, subject to a cycle of life, death, and resurrection. We look at the spider

> **The power that makes grass grow, fruit ripen, and guides the bird in flight is in us all.**
>
> *Anzia Yezierska*

with new eyes in the spiritual garden; her shimmering web set among the branches and flowers makes it clear why she was a symbol of the divine weaver who made the world, and why, unmoving in the web, she was thought to be a mysterious creature of the moon, feminine in nature. She—like the bee, the earth-

worm, and the garden's other creatures—seems perfectly, miraculously crafted for what she needs to do in life. Her spinnerets produce threads full of protein which harden as they are drawn out to form silk. These silken threads are amazing multipurpose tools for spinning webs, trapping prey, constructing egg sacs and cocoons; they even provide a form of transportation for a short drop down onto a flower or, spun as a gossamer thread, a vehicle

From opposite left to right: *Each of the garden's denizens is an emblem of spirit: the carp, or koi, stands for a long, fulfilled life; the frog for rebirth. The bird is a messenger between earth and heaven; the butterfly symbolizes the undying soul; and the spider and its web signify Creator and creation.*

perfect for ballooning, sending spiderlings afloat for long distances on the wind. Watching the spider drop its silken thread seems a testimony to divine intent.

Unseen, in the soil beneath our fingers, the pattern of relationship is no less complicated or awe-inspiring, a cycle of life, death, and renewal played out on a miniature scale that belies its importance. In conjunction with mites, millipedes, beetles, and earthworms, microscopic living organisms—nematodes, protozoa, fungi, and threadlike bacteria called actinomycetes—feed on dead and dying plant and animal matter and transform it metabolically and chemically into simpler components. These organic compounds are absorbed by plant roots and cells for growth. The soil literally teems with microorganisms; it has been estimated that a single gram of fertile soil contains no fewer than 100 million bacteria. Bacteria are literally ubiquitous; they can be found in the bodies of all living organisms and on every part of the planet we call home—in the depths of the ocean and on land, in the boiling water of hot springs and in the ice of arctic glac-

iers. Microbes are a large part of the web of relationship called life in the garden and, as we garden, they are our constant companions.

The spiritual garden teaches us about the limitations of "ownership." While the deeds we hold to our properties declare "possession," the act of gardening teaches us that there is a larger sense in which the earth we dig "belongs" to no one and everyone. We are just guardians of our plots of earth and, by extension, guardians of all the creatures who live in and around it. And with guardianship comes responsibility, and another lesson in community. We can acknowledge our stewardship to the butterflies and birds by planting for them, and they in turn will reward us by calling our gardens home.

Not every lesson the garden teaches is an easy one, and the hardest spiritual test may be learning to live with the unwelcome guest in the garden. Rabbits, chipmunks, moles, and, especially deer are capable of inflicting—from a human point of view—a tremendous amount of damage to the garden. From their standpoint,

of course, they are simply doing what they do: browsing and foraging to survive and building homes for themselves and their kin.

THE GARDENER AS GUARDIAN:
ORGANIC GARDENING

The most important lesson in reciprocity for the spiritual gardener is more complicated than the simple gesture of planting flowers and bushes for birds and butterflies. Understanding what it means to be a steward—from the Old English, a keeper of a yard, enclosure, or garden—requires that we first understand what a garden is. And for all that gardening does do to put us in touch with the cycles of life and the seasons, nonetheless we need to acknowledge an all-important fact: There is nothing "natural" about a garden. (As Maggie Oster, writer, photographer, and horticulturist, notes, even when we vary what we plant, "the garden is still closer to a monoculture, and a long way from nature.") There is nothing in the natural world that remotely resembles a garden; the garden—like its closest relative in nature, the meadow—requires maintenance or intervention to sustain itself. As Ken Druse writes in *The Natural Shade Garden*, "Even the meadow, in order to stay meadow, must be cut down once a year by fire, drought, or man. The forest does quite well on its own, for nature favors the woodland most of all."

Spiritual gardening requires that, even as we garden, we commit to disturbing the web of life as little as possible. Any alteration to any part of the web reverberates elsewhere, as the last 30 years—with its sad narrative of ecological disaster—has taught us. What has come to be called "organic gardening" has grown out of the commitment of many gardeners to limit the number and kind of significant changes they make to the soil, the water supply, and the living organisms in the garden. This commitment—which includes limiting or foreswearing the use of

chemicals and pesticides and substituting alternative ways of coping with pest control in the garden—is central to spiritual gardening, regardless of the type of sanctuary you create. The precepts of organic gardening are drawn from the model nature provides, using nature's own balance of beneficial and predatory insects and its built-in cycle of renewal and decay, as well as alternative, organic insecticides and soil enrichments. (For more specific information on organic gardening, see page 173.)

Above: *California natives,* **Iris Douglasiana** *and* **Limanthes douglasii,** *enrich a garden of spirit devoted to honoring the earth.*

Opposite: *Companion planting has been made part of this organic garden; the interspersed marigolds repel insects from the surrounding greens.*

the owner's skill, good taste, and financial status. Spiritual gardening has another goal entirely. As Maggie Oster puts it, "Gardening makes you humble. We each are cursed with the fantasy of perfection—the perfect border or even the perfect Zen garden but nature confounds us at every turn. On a basic level, gardening teaches simple lessons about control, about the ephemeral quality of life, about the forces of nature because there is no stasis in the garden." Our informed acknowledgment of the web of life is an important step toward spiritual growth.

MAKING ROOM FOR THE SOUL

Your garden, regardless of the form it takes, is the visible symbol of your commitment to making room for the spirit in everyday life. And that com-

mitment is the "single step" of the journey to which Lao Tzu refers. It doesn't matter whether you choose to use your garden as a place of individual retreat or one where you honor and celebrate the ties of family and community, as one family did in the northeast in memory of their son. The spiritual exercise of the garden may take the form of weeding as well as planting, as it did for Jami Lin, an internationally known designer and feng shui author and consultant. She recalls how, at the beginning of her own journey toward spirit, she would work in the garden, observing its cycles. Her own spiritual epiphany took place when, working without gloves, her hands came upon an earthworm, part of, as she puts it, "the living and nurturing soil." She understood her gardening

While the widespread use of pesticides in agriculture during the nineteenth and twentieth centuries was in part an answer to the requirements of a growing population, the contemporary use of pesticides in the home garden—which is no longer needed to fulfill a family's basic needs—is dictated by the desire for bigger, better, more "foolproof" flowers, fruits, and vegetables and a vision of the garden as yet another "well-decorated room" that reflects

> The tree which fills the arms grew from the tiniest sprout . . . the journey of a thousand miles commenced with a single step.
>
> *Lao Tzu*

work as "planting seeds of opportunity, planting seeds of heart."

Specific rites of devotion can also be a part of spiritual gardening. The garden designed for Richard Riordan, the mayor of Los Angeles, by architect James Heaton III and landscape architect Dennis Kurutz, is a place of respite and meditation. At its center, amid the surrounding lawn, rose garden, and fruit trees, is

Opposite top: *In Jami Lin's feng shui garden, a fire ritual performed at each new moon conveys blessings upon friends and clients.*

Opposite bottom: *Ritual purification is a part of all spiritual traditions; here, in a Zen garden, a water basin and spout mark the journey into sacred space.*

Right: *Chris Jacobson's altar includes a lion's head fountain as well as fragrant herbs, stones, and other found objects, and is the garden's focal point visible from the garden and the dining room.*

a private chapel; built in the timber and stone Italian Renaissance style of the main house, the chapel will accommodate six to eight people. It is filled with Catholic icons and statuary, including an image of St. Francis; three niches, symbolic of the Trinity, grace its walls. The land has been deliberately graded upward behind the chapel to encourage the growth of moss and algae and has made the building look mottled with age, like a centuries-old European chapel. All around the periphery of the property is a meditation trail; this path is made of decomposed granite in one area, then becomes a grass walk near a lily pond, a mossy area in another, and, close to the chapel, a stone walk. Nestled within an arbor of wisteria is a teak meditation bench. Other features of the garden—a hidden gate, the ruins of

a circular tower—add to a deliberate sense of mystery that is an essential part of this beautifully designed spiritual garden. The sacred spaces Barrie Kavasch, a horticulturist, herbalist, writer, and artist, has created draw on a different spiritual tradition, that of Native America; the medicine wheel gardens she has designed for public view at the Institute for American Indian Studies and for her personal use invite a different kind of participation. As Barrie points out, if there is a single thread that links all of the diverse Native American peoples, it is what she calls "the dance of reciprocity," the ritual gestures of giving thanks for the bounty of nature. The Institute's medicine wheel garden, an eastern medicine wheel facing west, is designed with areas symbolic of the four cardinal directions. As is tra-

("Lasting Peace" in Delaware), and *Wowalj'w* ("Peace" in Lakota). The base of the peace pole is a "growing" prayer cairn of stones—continually increasing and changing as visitors enter the garden and place stones on it, along with their prayers for peace. (A cairn—a deliberately placed pile of rocks or pebbles—is perhaps the oldest human marker of sacred space, and the practice of building cairns is common to every continent on which human beings have lived since prehistory, when cairns marked burial sites.) Upturned logs behind the garden provide a place to sit, and, as Barrie tells it, visitors to the Institute, regardless of their personal religious beliefs or commitments, are drawn to participate in the sacred space. "The whole garden is an altar," she notes, and the regular addition to and resetting of the stones in the cairns has given the medicine wheel garden a special sanctity, something she attributes to "the accumulated energy of prayer over time."

Both of Barrie's personal medicine wheel gardens are shaped out of earth, encouraging her to "read the landscape on a practical and spiritual alignment." The larger of the two gardens is a sanctuary, more like a Japanese meditation space in feeling; at its center is a cairn of tiny white stones. She brought moss into the earthworks, which is also home to Native American healing herbs, such as skullcap, speedwell, sweetgrass, and jewelweed. The second sacred space is mounded with an altar and peace pole at its center and rimmed by hazelnut, witch hazel, and bayberry. Here she feels the natural invasion of certain plants—such as poke—occurs to teach her to pay attention to reciprocity in the landscape and learn from it.

ditional for some tribes, each of the four directions is aligned with a color, and has color-appropriate plantings.

More than 30 species of healing plants make up this sacred garden, planted within a 30-foot-diameter circle of stones: The east is represented by gold and yellow blossoming plants, the west by red and orange, blue and purple for the south, and white, cream, and silver as emblems of the north. At the wheel's center is a peace pole on which the word "peace" is written in four Native American languages: *Onen* ("Peace be with you" in Iroquois), *Aquene* ("Peace" in Southeastern Algonquin), *Achwangundowagan*

Both the design and use of sacred space are processes that draw on both the conscious and unconscious levels of mind and spirit. We learn as we create and we change as we garden. Let the process inform your spirit.

Sacred space can be created with the simplest of gestures—a single camellia placed in a niche (above)—or can be part of a grander scheme, such as the rose bower on the page opposite.

The Spiritual Gardens

The garden and I have a relationship
which means that, the longer it goes on
the more I surround myself
with mental space and,
should I want it, self-discovery.

Mirabel Osler

CREATING THE SANCTUARY GARDEN

Designing sacred space outdoors is a creative process that draws on all of our inner resources and both our conscious and unconscious thoughts and associations. The idea of "process" is important: Creating the spiritual garden will, in turn, change and enrich our perceptions and spiritual awareness.

Jaen Treesinger, a horticulturist and garden designer with over 20 years of experience, remarks that, "In the partnership with earth, you develop respect and understanding with every gardening task you perform, whether you are moving a rock or adding a plant. Designing a garden allows you to envision the future you want in positive ways; gardening lets you manifest that vision." She points out that while garden design focuses you on the future—seeing the garden in this season and imagining it in the next—it also connects you firmly to the details of the present, since plants are never static but always in a stage of growth or decline. Recounting the ways in which she has changed as a result of gardening, she signals out the personally most significant: her increased powers of observation; her acknowledgment of the potential in all things, based in the lessons of growth in the garden; her increased patience, since the cycle of nature cannot be sped up or slowed down. For Jaen, the planting of trees has particular spiritual resonance. Since the tree planted will almost certainly outlive her, it is a reminder of her own limits and mortality. Yet its continued presence on earth, after her, will nonetheless be a testament to her acts and ability to enhance the landscape.

The inspiration for creating a garden of spirit can be found in many different places. Pamela Woods, who now specializes in the design of sacred gardens, was trained as a botanist but found lab work unsatisfying. She became a landscape architect, but it wasn't until she spent a year traveling the world that the idea of the landscape as sacred was brought home to her. The transformative experience was at Ayers Rock in Australia, a place sacred to the indigenous peoples; there Pamela truly understood and saw, as if for the first time, "the earth as the belly and soul of the Mother." Upon her return to England, she embarked on a different kind of garden design, one that envisioned a fully collaborative process that would take into account the spirit of the land, plants, and trees and that of the steward of the garden. Each of the gardens she has designed is unique; Pamela understands the creation and design of outdoor sacred space as an opportunity for a person to articulate his or her relationship to the earth, and to clarify personal intentions by creating a place to experience the spirit within.

Sometimes the workings of a world marked by violence can provide the starting point for a sanctuary, as it did for Emil Miland and Fred Sonenberg. Their 30-foot-square garden, in the common courtyard they share with their neighbors Cindy and Christopher Burt in San Francisco, was created in response to the American bombing of Baghdad. Emil was horrified by the war, broadcast live into America's living rooms, and the garden was conceived and created as a private protest for peace, using symbolism drawn from Tibetan Buddhism. What was originally a square cement patio was transformed into a garden in the shape of a mandala—a circle within a square—with pieces of the salvaged concrete used as pavers. At the very center of the garden is a fountain, designed by Fred and inspired by a Tibetan wall hanging that contains a series of concentric circles; at the center is a ring of human skulls. The fountain, made of poured concrete, is set with Indonesian turquoise rocks; in the water are rocks carved to resemble skulls, serving as momento mori. There are statues in the garden, among them a Kuan Yin, the Chinese goddess of mercy, and two seated terra-cotta figures from Java; a hand of Buddha blesses the garden from a stairwell perch. The experience of collaborating on the design of this garden has been important to both men and their relationship. While serving for

The ten different sanctuary gardens on the pages following can be used as templates to create your own sacred space or simply as sources of inspiration. Be guided by your own vision of the design vocabulary that best articulates the presence of the sacred for you and by how you intend to use your garden of spirit. The following suggestions may be of help as you plan:

• Experience the property you intend to cultivate at various times of day. Discover the areas in which you feel most comfortable, and oberve both the amount and strength of sunlight those areas receive.

• Survey the existing plantings, and decide which elements you want to integrate into your garden of spirit.

• Ask yourself which of your five senses connects you most readily to spirit. You need to know yourself before you plan and plant.

• Remember that creating a garden of spirit is highly personal, and that there are no "rules" to follow. Feel free to use elements from different traditions if you wish.

Marcia and Jack Kelly, who have visited more than 250 places of retreat and sanctuary in the United States in the course of writing their books, remind us that location and size have little to do with the feeling of a garden sanctuary; they have experienced the tranquillity of sanctuary gardens in the inner-city courtyard of a monastery as well as in formal gardens, set on rolling hills, in the countryside. As Marcia puts it, all these sanctuaries permit us "to step away from the world, and allow us to enjoy the bounties of earth and heavens." Jack adds that "the visual beauty of a garden heightens our awareness of the things we overlook in the daily busyness of our lives outside." Crossing the threshold of the garden or passing through its gates, we sense a calm emanating, as Marcia and Jack put it, "from the prayers and spiritual practices that imbue the landscape and radiate out from it."

That calm can be made a part of your everyday life as well.

both of them as an oasis in a crowded urban environment, the garden has taught them different lessons. Emil, a gardener since childhood and a cellist by profession, begins each day in the garden; it is, he says, a "chance for a moment of repose." The garden fulfills his need "to get his hands in the earth" and to connect to the life cycle. For Fred, the garden has been a place to recover from heart surgery; designing and working in the garden, he's been able to give himself permission "simply to enjoy."

Above: *A place of sanctuary can be simplicity itself: here, a stone pagoda, shaded by bamboo, flanked by a wood railing.*

THE *Tranquillity* GARDEN

If you love truth, be a lover of silence.

Silence like the sunlight

will illuminate you in God ...

Thomas Merton

 If there is anything that characterizes most of our lives, it is the day-long bombardment of stimuli. From the moment our alarms go off in the morning to the time we turn off the lights at night and only the hum of the refrigerator remains, we are surrounded by sound—cars honking, people talking, phones and faxes ringing, children clamoring, a steady background of radio and television. Smells envelop us—from the exhaust of cars to a stranger's perfume or the wafting airs from a sidewalk food cart. The lights of the office, the glare of the computer screen, and the insistent barrage of brightly colored graphics everywhere we look dull our eyes to visual pleasure. Most of us have learned to "tune out" whenever we can. But of course, tuning out doesn't mean that we aren't being affected. It simply means we've chosen not to be aware of how much our spirit is affected by uninvited influences.

The tranquillity garden is a place of retreat from the cacophony of the world, based on principles that emphasize balance and calm, not abundant stimulation. Its color sense is deliberately muted and emphasizes the harmonious blending of shades. Remember that bright, bold colors—vibrant reds and purples—are filled with energy and agitate, rather than calm; for sacred space, focus instead on the natural greenery of certain plants—angelica or the shade-loving hosta, for example—to give it its special character. Look to paler shades in your plantings—soft creams and pastels—to induce a feeling of serenity. Under ideal circumstances, the tranquillity garden is partly shaded and the corner of your yard unsuited for plants which need full sun may be the perfect spot—this is a garden that welcomes the soft growth of moss, dappled in sunlight and deep velvet in shade. Moss, one of the planet's most ancient plants, is a visual reminder of the continuities that underlie all the energy and change surrounding us.

The symbolism of this sacred space is deliberately grounded: This is a garden that can make use of the immutability and permanence of rock to signify the grounded nature of larger truths and principles, or the presence of a deity in everyday life. Yet motion—the soft energy of the wind rustling the trees or moving the fronds of a fern—is also an aid to the meditative mood the garden evokes. Our English word "meditation" is inadequate to describe the many techniques offered by different spiritual traditions to help connect with the sacred, but most

Previous pages: *The serenity of still waters, graced by lotus blossoms at Lotusland in Santa Barbara, California, spills over onto the visitor's soul.*

Above left: *A serpentine path, surrounded by rye, leads to the meditation garden at Chanticleer, a former estate. The deliberately muted tones in the plantings encourage the viewer to focus on texture and shape.*

Above: *A stone bench in a city garden provides a safe haven for body and soul amid the bustle of everyday life.*

Opposite: *In this sanctuary, a simple bench becomes a place for thought and meditation, sheltered by flowering vines.*

assume that we need to let go of the "now" before we are able to connect spiritually. In Zen Buddhism the meditative techniques all emphasize separation from the world, whether the *zazen*—sitting with legs fully or half crossed, in a quiet place, breathing rhythmically and maintaining silence, freed of all desire—or the *koan*, a contemplation of the paradox or puzzle that cannot be understood through conventional thought. (For more, see page 98.) In Tibetan Buddhism, visualization of the sacred—in the form of the mandala—is an aid to understanding that the sacred is indistinguishable from everyday reality; you may wish to incorporate a symbolic mandala, such as a single flower, a water lily in a small pond, or a group of flowers. In the various Christian traditions, separation from the world and immersion in spirit are achieved both through silence and through contemplation of either a mystery of faith or a passage of Scripture. (Thomas Merton, a Trappist monk, wrote in his book *Contemplative Prayer*: "The contemplative waits in silence and when he is 'answered,' it is not so much by a word that bursts into his silence. It is by this silence itself suddenly, inexplicably, revealing itself to him as a word of great power.") Remember that, generally, meditation is deep, sustained thought, free of other distractions. Meditation is not goal-oriented and should not be confused with problem-solving or thinking something "through." If anything, meditation is deliberately nonlinear in nature; it is reflective, closed, and continuous. In this garden, closed off from everyday distractions, the soft sounds of wind and water may help us to "hear" in the silence. While there are sacred spaces that encourage us to meditate through movement and activity (see the "The Zen Garden," page 98, and "The Labyrinth Garden," page 156), in the tranquillity garden letting go of our need to act, do, and accomplish is part of the spiritual exercise. In this garden, a path is introduced as a purely symbolic element, existing only as a visual reminder that true spiritual energy is based in tranquillity.

If you have room in your garden, you can create a path amid your plantings or, if space is at a premium, simply place a rock or two to indicate the presence of the path in your life. One woman who created a tranquillity garden on her small terrace collected rounded stones and placed them amid her potted plants and her small fountain. On each stone she wrote words that recalled the values she needed to honor in her sacred space: "awareness," "thoughtfulness," "mercy."

As you consider the design of your sacred space dedicated to serenity, resist the urge to incorporate a large variety of plantings. In many traditions, deliberate repetition underlies some of the most effective methods of clearing the mind and soul of excess—the chant, the mantra, or the recitation of a rosary, for example. Repeated elements in the garden can act as a visual mantra; the simplicity of color, texture, and variety contributes to the feeling of peace the space inspires in us.

Consider incorporating the element of water into your tranquillity garden, something you can do on a very small scale. The sound of flowing water soothes the soul and relaxes the body; it purifies and cleanses. My friend Leslie built a small water garden by sinking a traditional half whiskey barrel into the ground, first lining it with heavy-duty plastic to prevent leakage. Her water garden didn't even need a filtration system, since it included parrot's feather, an oxygenating plant; fairy moss and duckweed, two floating plants, provided the needed shade to cut down on the growth of algae in the still water. She then added two marginals—plants which in nature sit on the edges of bodies of water—taro and zebra grass, as well as two small water lilies. Two gold-fish not only provided visual interest and energy to the water but disposed of the larvae mosquitoes would lay on the water's surface. Nestled in the corner of her backyard by an old weathered wooden bench, under the branches of a rose of Sharon, her water garden is a perfect oasis at the end of a busy day. (For more on creating water fea-tures, see page 171.)

As you choose plantings for this space, consider scent as well; once again, you're looking for smells that relax, rather than stimulate, to maintain the sense of balance and uninterruptedness that a sanctuary devoted to quiet and meditation requires. Unless a plant has specific per-sonal associations that are restorative (recalling a place where you truly felt at ease, for example), try to stay away from heavy scents such as honeysuckle or lilac which will perfume the air.

The garden of tranquillity—no matter how large or small—should be set off from the bustle of the day. If you're working on a patio or a small deck, look beyond where you plan to set your containers and make sure that the outside world doesn't impinge upon you through the view. Think about how you'll use the space you've created: Do you need a small bench or will you sit among the plants? Remember the lessons of the Zen and Eastern gar-dens; if there isn't enough room for you to sit among the plants, then you can site your sacred space so it can be viewed from inside your home.

If you are creating an area devoted to tranquillity within a larger garden or on a corner of your property, choose a spot that is out of the way of the outdoor activi-ties you and your family enjoy; it should, ideally, be set off from neighboring yards by either a fence or a natural sep-aration such as a hedge. A tranquillity garden is a place

where we try to reap the healing benefits of solitude and quiet. A tranquillity garden need not be a garden in the traditional sense; a bench placed on a moss-covered bit of shaded ground beneath the branches of a tree will suffice.

PLANTING FOR TRANQUILLITY

If you keep it small and plant it with care, your tranquillity garden can become the one place in your life where there is little in the way of unfinished business and everything is trimmed to a soft edge. In a tranquillity garden we create a

Above: *A sheltered bench in an English garden is a place of retreat, set off from the world outside by hedges and plantings.*

Opposite: *The meditation garden at Mount Calvary in Santa Barbara, California, is deliberately enclosed, set off from worldly distractions. At its center is a cross, emblem of the Christian faith and of Christ's presence.*

space where we can concentrate on inner thoughts rather than on unpulled weeds or errant branches. The actual work of gardening isn't part of the spiritual discipline of this particular sacred space; manageability is the first requirement.

If you can, site your tranquillity garden in an area with an existing separation, such as a hedge or fence. If no such separation is available, you can create one with conifers like Japanese yew (*Taxus cuspidata*) or American arborvitae (*Thuja occidentalis*). Trees up to five feet tall can be purchased inexpensively at most garden centers; planted three

to four feet apart, most large conifers will form a solid wall, six to seven feet tall, in just a few years. They require minimum care, other than shaping once or twice a season. An arbor or fence—particularly one that can support climbing plants—could also form the necessary division for your tranquillity garden.

Once you've defined your space, think carefully about what goes into it. As you consider the visual effect of each plant and how it will combine with other plants in the garden, think, too, about caring for it, since high maintenance is not

part of the exercise of this spiritual garden. Space your plants generously; crowded plants give a more immediate effect but require more care in the long run.

Ask about the vigor of each plant you're considering. A fast-growing perennial ground cover like English ivy (*Hedera helix*) or snow-on-the-

Water: life-giving, purifying, regenerative.

Above: *In the Penick family garden in Virginia, a bench under the branches of a weeping willow offers a view of a quiet lake, making a place conducive to the work of the soul.*

mountain (*Euphorbia marginata*) provides quick coverage, and a solid mat of a single plant allows you to concentrate on focal points in containers or other areas. But the most vigorous plants will also crowd out

Right: *A pond filled with water lilies conveys a vision of spirit which has been known to humanity for thousands of years, and connects us, symbolically and literally, to all those who have walked the earth before us.*

Above: *The smallest of terra-cotta fountains, set amid hostas, lends both a soothing sound and soft energy to this tiny tranquillity garden on a terrace.*

others, and the work of eradicating them can turn your place of retreat into a space filled with effort. If you wish to create a varied, textured landscape, choose plants that are more refined in their growth habits. Even annual plants such as coleus can become problematic when they set seed and regrow year after year.

If you plan on using your garden all year long, keep in mind how a given plant will change over the course of the seasons. A variegated iris might serve as a focal point in mid-spring; later in summer its exquisite striped foliage remains eyecatching amid the greenery of the garden. The delicate blossoms of a Siberian dogwood shrub (*Cornus alba* 'Siberica') grace the early spring garden; in winter the shrub's fiery red twigs stand out against

> **Whatever peace I know rests in the natural world, in feeling myself a part of it, even in a small way.**
>
> *May Sarton*

snow. Ever-greens (your conifer hedge, for example) are attractive in every season, and have the added advantage of potent symbolism; they are emblems of immortality and endurance.

Consider using vines in your tranquillity garden. Among the most useful are Boston ivy (*Parthenocissus tricuspidata*), a clinging deciduous

vine with large glossy-green leaves that turn red in autumn; and fiveleaf akebia (*Akebia quinata*), a vigorous evergreen vine that produces intensely fragrant lavender flowers, followed by fruit pods in the fall. Perennial plants that return year after year are also good choices. Consider lady's mantle (*Alchemilla mollis*), with scalloped bright green foliage that can be positioned to spill over containers or borders; it bears chartreuse flowers in spring or early summer. And don't forget hostas, which range from small to huge, and are valued for their leaves, which can be blue, green, gray, gold, or variegated in exquisite patterns. Most require some shade, though a few will tolerate sunny conditions. Solomon's seal (*Polygonatum odoratum*), ornamental grasses, and ferns also add interest in the tranquillity garden.

Right: *In this tranquillity garden, the path lined with bamboo yields to a simple bench for rest and reflection.*

Opposite left: *A single flower can become a mandala for meditation; here, a hybrid calendula acts as a symbol of the unity within multiplicity in the setting of the spiritual garden.*

Opposite far left: *Hostas and ferns in a garden designed by landscape architect Osamu Shimizu.*

THE *Healing* GARDEN

A wise man should consider that health

is the greatest of human blessings

and learn how by his own thoughts to derive

benefit from his illnesses.

Hippocrates

Among the gifts of the garden is its ability to heal body and soul. The healing garden is a place to acknowledge the degree to which our physical and spiritual balance is restored by being out in nature, and how the tasks of planting and tending, which connect us directly to the cycles of growth, are effective therapeutic tools. Jaen Treesinger, horticulturist and garden designer, notes that even the maintenance tasks of the garden—weeding, deadheading, raking—have repetitive aspects similiar to certain spiritual practices of prayer and meditation, such as reciting a mantra or using a rosary. In the garden, Jaen notes, these tightly focused tasks, like meditation practices, "create structure and boundaries which permit us to free our creative aspects."

In this sacred space we also honor the living earth as the source of humanity's first pharmacopoeia. No one knows when we first discovered that plants could help sustain life, but it must have been early in human

history. We don't know with any certainty how human beings first learned about the healing power of plants; perhaps the earliest hunters watched as animals foraged, and observed firsthand how different plants affected them. Even an animal's continued avoidance of a specific plant would have taught an important lesson. Finally, both accidental human ingestion and deliberate trial and error probably also contributed to what was, for thousands of years, a powerful bounty for humanity, representing infor-

Above: *At Avena Botanicals in Rockport, Maine healing herbs are grown in a beautifully designed patchwork garden, surrounded by a circular path.*

Previous pages: *At the Hermitage of the Dayspring, in Kent, Connecticut, there is a special garden meant to heal the heart and soul. Designed as a raked sand meditation garden, it was intended to memorialize priests and brothers who died of AIDS but its power to soothe the ravages of the heart soon extended to others who have suffered grievous loss. Around the "sea" of raked stone are flowering trees and shrubs donated as memorials.*

mation so precious that it was known only to a few in each community. These few—the healers, shamans, and priests—were guardians of nature's pharmacopoeia, and there seems little question that the magical qualities and the ritual use associated with plants in ancient cultures were inseparable from their medicinal value.

The healing properties of plants added another dimension to the spiritual acknowledgment of humanity's dependence on the landscape, which already supplied food, water, and shelter. In every ancient culture, the curative power of plants was attributed to the intervention of supernatural powers. In Egypt, healing was the gift of the sun god Ra; in the lands settled by the Phoenicians it came from Eshmumun; the ancient Greeks left offerings in the temple of Asclepius, whose stick of intertwined snakes—the caduceus—is still a symbol of medicine. In Hinduism the bael tree or Bengal quince, an important medicinal, was sacred to both Lakshmi, the goddess of wealth, and Shiva, the god of healing, and was planted near temples. In ancient Egypt, the preparation of herbal medicines was always accompanied by ritual incantation: "O Isis, great enchantress, free me, release me from all evil red things, from the fever of the god and the fever of the goddess." Similarly, ingesting the medicine also required the patient's ritual participation: "Come, remedy, drive it out of my heart, out of these my limbs, strong in magic power with the remedy." In the Americas shamans cured both the physical body and the soul touched by malignant influences through an inseparable combination of herbal remedies, ritual dance, prayer, and gestures of thankfulness. According to E. Barrie Kavasch in her book *Native Harvests*, the root was the part of the plant most used by the Indians, although they used bark and leaf as well. They were expert harvesters, digging different roots at the optimal moment in the plant's cycle: the roots of annuals were harvested in the spring before the plant's flowering while those of biennials and perennials were gathered in

autumn, when they were rich in stored nutrients. Among the many native plants used for medicinal purposes were borage (*Borago officinalis*) to reduce fever; various clovers

Above: *A traditional English physic garden is planted with poppies, rue, foxglove, boxwood, and holly.*

Right: *This beautiful healing garden is planted with alliums, oregano, and phlox. Alliums or onions have been used the world over for treating a variety of illnesses, among them colds and coughs, while oregano, now prized for its culinary use, was an important medicinal herb for the ancient Greeks. The leaves of phlox, native to the American continent but introduced into Europe, were used for skin disorders and gastric distress.*

91

(*Trifolium* sp.) for salves to treat sores and ulcer; dandelion (*Taraxacum officinale*) for digestive ailments; comfrey (*Symphytum officinale*) for bruises and damaged tissues; and corn (*Zea mays*), used by the Incas and Aztecs to cure bladder and kidney infections.

The knowledge and use of healing plants evolved in different ways

Left: *Here in the Rudolf Steiner Fellowship Foundation garden, yarrow, dill, and roses combine to create a place to heal both body and soul. Yarrow* (Achillea millefolium) *was long known to heal wounds, while dill* (Anethum graveolens) *is an aromatic herb, used medicinally for thousands of years; its name comes from the Norse, meaning "to soothe." Aconite, planted in the foreground, is beautiful but highly toxic.*

from culture to culture, often closely connected to visions of spirit as well as to an understanding of the human body. What was once an oral tradition of healing became, in different civilizations, part of the written word as early as 5,000 years ago, and perhaps even earlier. Ayurveda, the healing system of the Indian subcontinent (its name means "science of life"), is probably the oldest; it survives in earliest written form in the *Vedas,* Sanskrit poetry dating from 1500 B.C.; the *Rigveda* contains a list of more than 1,000 medicinal plants. Ayurveda is a holistic system incorporating spirit, mind, and body; it posits the existence of seven energy centers in the body (*chakras*), and Ayurvedic medicine restores balance through herbal treatment and mental and physical

exercises called yogas. The Egyptian *Ebers Papyrus,* which is roughly contemporaneous with the *Vedas,* devotes almost equal space to its medicinal herbs—some 800 of them, including anise, caraway, coriander, saffron, and mustard—and to incantations. In China the art of healing with plants was also well established, though its written form, *The Yellow Emperor's Classic,* is probably later in date than its Egyptian and Indian counterparts. The Chinese tradition, too, is holistic, involving both body and spirit; in conjunction with herbal remedies, medical practitioners used massage, acupuncture, and exercise.

In the European West, medicine became gradually deritualized and separated from supernatural influences; the Greek Hippocrates,

popularly known as the "father of Western medicine," who lived in the fifth century B.C., examined the causes of disease, among them diet and environment, rather than attributing illness to the intervention of the gods. Western medical practices were profoundly influenced by his writings as they were by those of Dioscorides, the first-century Greek doctor whose treatise *De materia medica,* a listing of some 600 plants and their medicinal properties, would be the standard textbook along with the work of Galen, who

From far left to right: *The aptly named feverfew* (Chyrsanthemum parthenium)*; angelica* (Angelica archangelica)*; purple coneflower* (Echinacea purpurea)*, one of the most important medicinal herbs; and agave* (Agave americana)*, used by the Mayans and Aztecs for wounds.*

Above: *While* Rosa gallica *is not much used in herbal medicine today, it has a long medicinal history, and its essential oil is used in aromatherapy treatments as an antidepressant. The essential oil should only be used internally under professional supervision.*

was court physician to Marcus Aurelius, for the next 1,700 years. The authority accorded these ancient texts had the unwanted effect of discouraging new medical investigation in the West for the same period of time as well.

Before planting a healing garden, whether you are using it simply as a place of sanctuary that connects you to another aspect of the planet's gifts or for medicinal use, it is crucial to acknowledge that plants are every bit as powerful and as inherently dangerous to your health as prescription drugs taken without the advice of a physician. Under no circumstances should you self-prescribe. Be aware that many plants are toxic, and still others are potentially dangerous if taken in incorrect dosages. Many herbs are contraindicated for pregnant women and, in general, pregnant women should not use any herbs in any form, either internally or externally, without the advice of a health care practitioner. In addition, in a garden that will be visited by children and pets, keep in mind that certain plants, despite their herbal history and any medicinal claims that may be made for them, should be deliberately excluded for reasons of safety. A very partial list of the plants which, if accidentally ingested, are potentially very dangerous might include autumn crocus (*Colchicum autumnale*); deadly nightshade (*Atropa belladonna*); aconite (*Aconitum* sp.), a beautiful but very toxic plant, for all of its parts are poisonous; blue cohosh (*Caulophyllum thalictroides*); German chamomile (*Chamomilla recutita*) since contact with the plant can cause dermatitis; goldenseal (*Hydrastis canadensis*); rue (*Ruta gravolens*); foxglove (*Digitalis purpurea*); peony (*Paeonia* sp.); and opium poppy (*Papaver somniferum*). If you have any questions or doubts about the potential toxicity of a plant, even if you have no intentions of harvesting it for medicinal use, please consult your local garden center, your local poison-control center, or the Centers for Disease Control in Atlanta, Georgia, for more information.

You might want to create a small garden that symbolically honors the healing properties of plants, and adds color and beauty to your sacred space at the same time. Among the plants to consider are angelica (*Angelica archangelica*), long used as a panacea and so named because it blooms on the archangel Michael's feast day (who, legend has it, appeared in a vision to explain the herb's healing properties); dill (*Anethum graveolens*), which was listed in the *Ebers Papyrus* and was, for thousands of years, considered soothing to the stomach; purple coneflower (*Echinacea purpurea*), an important part of Native American medicine and known to be an immune stimulant; aloe (*Aloe vera*) which

Above: *At the City of Hope in Duarte, California, this Japanese-style healing garden, used by patients, visitors, and staff, was created to provide a safe haven from the outside world, a place of rest and peace. The garden was designed by landscape architect Takeo Uesugi.*

Cleopatra is said to have favored as a skin conditioner and is an excellent home remedy for sunburn; garlic (*Allium sativum*); rosemary (*Rosmarinus officinalis*), traditionally used to strengthen memory; pot marigold (*Calendula officinalis*), which was used by the ancient Egyptians for medicinal purposes and still decorates Hindu altars; St. John's wort (*Hypericum perforatum*), a pretty plant once considered an effective repellent against witches and now recognized as an antidepressant (although one that may cause sun sensitivity); feverfew (*Chrysanthemum parthenium*), for its color, beauty, and name; and lemon balm (*Melissa officinalis*). For more on medicinal plants, see the Bibliography, page 186.

The degree to which human beings are healed by their involvement both with gardens and gardening, as well as the natural landscape, has been acknowledged in different ways all over the United States, at hospitals, hospices, and

Above and opposite: *English filmmaker, artist, and gay rights activist Derek Jarmon designed and worked in this sculpture garden, filled with plants and flowers and sculpture, after he learned he had AIDS. It was both a place of healing and of sanctuary, situated in a conservation area, in the shadow of a nuclear power station. Poles made of driftwood, gathered from the beach after storms, and found rocks and shells become sculptures in this seaside garden of spirit in the southeastern part of England.*

other institutions actively working to help patients recover from and cope with both physical and mental illness. An extraordinary symbolic landscape, a verdant therapeutic tool, was designed by landscape architect Douglas Reed at the Institute for Child and Adolescent Development in Wellesley, Massachusetts, with the guidance of its director, Dr. Sebastiano Santostefano. Dr. Santostefano calls the garden an "invaluable tool" for the process of therapy, for, as he puts it, "when a child engages the landscape, both the therapist and the child learn about and gain access to the child's inner world." This symbolic landscape is unified by a stream that runs through it, its source a granite basin that overflows slightly and entices the child to pursue the stream's progress through a symbolic landscape. Following the stream, the child encounters landscape features that are meant to elicit and clarify the child's responses to different situations: a stepping-stone "bridge" for risk-taking; a "cave," a bench under the branches of a yew for safety and enclosure; a "mount" for climbing; an "island," a thicket planted with swamp azalea, clethra, and shadblow; and, finally, an open area or "glade" for running and playing. By engaging the landscape, Dr. Santostefano notes, "body, soul,

and mind come together in ways that serve the child's development." He tells the story of a boy, now five, who came to the institute when he was just under three, after spending his early childhood enduring painful and lengthy hospitalizations. His withdrawal from the world was so complete that he was diagnosed as autistic, but Dr. Santostefano was convinced "that the soul and mind of the child had been locked up" and that he could be worked out of the position he had assumed toward an intrusive and painful world. Over the years the boy has literally and symbolically emerged from the therapeutic landscape, from hiding, wordless, in the "cave" to interacting with the trees and plants in the landscape, touching and watering them.

The healing garden can take on any number of aspects. It may be a place where the maintenance chores of the garden permit your mind to let go of the things that are bothering you, or it may simply be a place where, by planting beautiful herbs and flowers, you feel quiet in your soul. And then, too, for many of us, sitting at desks or working in front of computer screens all day, there is the simple kind of healing the garden brings: the pure pleasure of having our hands in the soil and the sun on our backs.

THE *Zen* GARDEN

Inside the sacred fence before which I bow

There must be a pond filled with clear water;

As my mind-moon becomes bright,

I see its shadow reflected in the water.

Daito Kokushi

Sacred space takes on the aspect of serenity in these stylized and symbolically rich gardens, which can provide the inspiration for distinctive home sanctuaries used for meditation or quiet retreat. The specific garden types that emerged and flourished on the islands of Japan—the stroll garden, the courtyard garden, the tea house garden, and the dry garden, among them—are the outgrowth of different traditions and sensibilities, some of them native and others borrowed from Chinese culture. Both the real topographies of China and Japan, their traditional cosmologies, and the legacies of Shintoism, Taoism and Zen Buddhism form a part of their symbolism and design. This spiritual tradition teaches us to see the elements of the landscape anew; here rock and pebble, water, tree and plant, and even

open space take on meanings very different from those in the Western tradition of symbolic landscape.

The serenity of these gardens is achieved through design principles based in the balance of yin and yang, or in their Japanese equivalents, *in* and *yo*. Their design is based on the balancing of opposites, expressed in the landscape: the stasis of rock set off against the fluidity of water; the pairing of the horizontal and the vertical; the linking of light and dark, and high and low, which allows each to be seen with clarity; the juxtaposition of sound, achieved by the rustle of grasses or falling water, with silence. Like the universe, of which it is both a part and a picture, the Japanese garden is dynamic and static at once. Change and

The cycles of time and season are expressed in the plantings and landscape of the Zen garden.

Above left: *In fall, at Asticou Garden, the changing leaf color, emblematic of change, is set against the permanence of stone, providing a visual metaphor for the universe's workings.*

Above: *At Shoyoan Teien, the Japanese Garden at Wesleyan University, the emergence that is spring is articulated by the crab apple blossom, limned against unchanging rock.*

Previous pages: *The relationship between interior and exterior space is central to the Japanese garden, as exemplified in the exquisite setting of the Hume Stroll Garden in Long Island, New York, designed by landscape architect Stephen Morrell.*

evolution find their expression in the planting of deciduous trees such as Japanese maple (*Acer palmatum*), Chinese redbud (*Cercis chinensis*), dogwood (*Cornus florida*), and flowering cherry and pear trees, traditional emblems of transience in both Japan and China, or shrubs, like Japanese quince (*Chaenomeles japonica*). Permanence, on the other hand, is suggested by evergreens such as Japanese red pine (*Pinus densiflora*) and shore pine (*Pinus contorta*), the presence of rock, and steady maintenance and pruning so that the garden retains its basic character from year to year, season to season.

The oldest and most sacred of Japanese gardens is not, to Western eyes, a garden at all. In the city of Ise, in the midst of a towering primeval forest near a river, stands a small wooden shrine with a bark roof dedicated to Ameratsu, the Shinto goddess of the sun and the national

Above: *The Zen garden expresses the journey that is life. The terraced path yields changing perspectives on the elements in the surrounding landscape. Here at the Cleveland Botanical Garden, the artifice that captures the essence of nature is evident in the rounded shapes of the shrubs and the careful selection and placement of rock.*

Two silken
moonstrands
Arc at the still
water's edge
Earthbound souls
aloft.

Anonymous

In China and Japan, because it was
thought to live for thousands of years,
the crane was a symbol of longevity
as well as faithfulness; its grace in
flight made it a potent symbol of
immortality, while its color signified
purity of spirit. It was thought, too,
that the crane transported the souls of
the dead to the Isles of the Immortals.
Here, at Hakone Japanese Gardens, a
statue of a crane completes a landscape
filled with serenity and grace.

103

guardian of Japan. The approach to the shrine takes the pilgrim—and there are thousands each year—through the forest, along graveled paths, through a series of gates (*torii*) as well as to a place of ablution. Although the pilgrim cannot enter the shrine, the approach—through gates as well as past rocks joined together by a woven rope representing sacred precincts—is a journey out of the secular into increasingly sacred space, of which the actual shrine forms only a part. Prayers and offerings are made outside of the shrine's gates. In Shintoism rocks, mountains, trees, and rivers are all revered as the loci of deities and, as if to underline how only the sacrality of nature is permanent, the man-made shrine to the goddess is ritually torn down and then rebuilt every 20 years.

The Shinto legacy of the sacred archetype underlies the importance of rocks in the Zen garden, although the symbolism ascribed to them would over time acquire more specific meaning. At the Raikyu-ji Temple garden, a cragged rock rises above smaller subsidiary rocks; it is the *shumisen*, the symbol of Mount Meru, the sacred mountain of Buddhist cosmology that was the center of the universe. The *shumisen*'s presence in the landscape is a visual shorthand for understanding the garden as the whole universe. The viewer is meant to look past the specifics in the landscape and to meditate instead on the aspect of truth embodied in it. The cosmological

Left: *The cascade of a waterfall, representing the continuous revewal of the spirit as well as the element of impermanence, brings movement and sound into the spiritual garden. The simple lines of the bridge contrast to the flow behind it; the bridge itself offers the visitor a place to pause and gain a new perspective on the landscape.*

scheme—which envisions eight concentric rings of mountain ranges radiating from Mount Meru, each separated by an ocean—is, in some Japanese gardens, represented in a more literal fashion, but the purpose is always the same. Garden design and sacred cosmology are one; the landscape doesn't represent the sacred story but, for the purposes of meditation, is the sacred story. Thus configurations of rocks, grouped in threes, focus the viewer's attention on the essential relationship of heaven, earth, and man, while another garden design might recreate a story drawn from Buddha's life. The Taoist vision of paradise—the story of the Mystical Islands of the Blessed—was another important subject for meditation in the garden, represented either by designing a pond with outcroppings of rock in a pond or, in a dry garden, by island-shaped areas of greenery amid gravel raked to represent water. In some cases the garden's design includes many details of the myth or story, such as differently shaped rocks to represent the turtles on which the islands rested or the cranes on which the immortals flew. In others the design is simplified so that the Taoist or Buddhist principle or story is demonstrated through a careful pattern of allusion. In his book *Japanese Gardens* Günter

Above: *In a private garden in Ohio, a simple, rough-hewn bench sits among stones, representing the river that is life, giving the vistor a place to meditate on the ever-changing nature of the world.*

Top: *Each rock in the Zen garden is carefully chosen for its texture, shape, and weatheredness and, then, is just as carefully and artfully placed.*

Nitschke analyzes the symbolism of the Daisen-in dry garden, the key to which is a single Bodhi tree, planted in the southwestern corner. The bodhi (*Ficus religiosa*) is the tree under which Buddha is said to have achieved enlightenment, and its presence, according to Nitschke, signals that

Above: *At Hakone Japanese Gardens in Saratoga, California, the serenity and harmony of all the elements in a varied landscape are beautifully realized.*

the entire garden is "a symbolic representation of the course of human life," expressed in carefully shaped configurations of rock and gravel, which symbolize a river of life proceeding from youth into maturity and, finally, old age.

The word "Zen" means "meditation" or "absorption," and all of these gardens are designed to aid in the process of enlightenment to which Zen is dedicated. The word "enlightenment," however—like the conception of nature— is used in a markedly different way here than it is in the

West, where it is closely associated with the acquisition of knowledge. In Zen teaching enlightenment (*satori*) does not proceed from the workings of intellect, as the fundamental Zen teaching tool, the *koan*, demonstrates, nor is it goal-oriented. It is instead a process of spiritual evolution. A *koan*—a phrase, meditation, or teaching—cannot be answered or understood by reason, as one of the most famous examples demonstrates: "What is the sound of one hand clapping?" Just as the form of the *koan* forces the student to set aside conventional ways of discursive understanding, so, too, the details of the Zen garden work to invite realization, deliberately breaking down the distinction between subject and object, viewer and that which is viewed.

A wonderful, if possibly apocryphal, anecdote is retold by Loraine Kuck in *The World of the Japanese Garden* illuminating both the philosophy of Zen Buddhism and its expression in garden design. Sen no Rikyu, a sixteenth-century tea master, designed and built a tea garden for a temple that had a magnificent view of Japan's Inland Sea. To everyone's surprise, including that of his students, he planted two tall hedges that obscured the view entirely. It was only when a guest bent over the stone basin in the garden to wash and purify his hands before the tea ceremony that he could glimpse the ocean through a small gap in the hedges. At that moment he understood that the small amount of water in the basin and the seemingly limitless sea were of the same substance and spirit; just as the waters were one so, too, were he and the the Infinite Universe. In the words of Sojo, a Zen monk and scholar: "Heaven and earth and I are of the same root." *Satori* involves full realization of that which already exists—the Buddha-nature of all things—and can thus be experienced through any number of concrete experiences in the garden, such as drawing water, raking sand, walking through a landscape, or sitting on a bench.

What underlies all of the types of Japanese gardens is the idea of "journey," although once again the journey does not imply, as it does in the West, a destination or the achievement of a specific goal. Instead it is a journey of progressive revelation, where the individual can, in Edward Hall's words, "discover something for himself." Thus, in the Japanese stroll garden, the landscape reveals itself slowly, by turns, encouraging the viewer's mindfulness as parts of it come into view. The details of the landscape—the outlines of a bridge reflected in water, soft shadows, the bright burst of color on a flowering tree, the sound of a waterfall, or the velvety texture of moss on stone—all are meant, singly and collectively, to represent the constantly evolving nature of the universe. The design technique usually referred to as "borrowed landscape" also contributes to the continuous sense of discovery provided the viewer in the garden. "Borrowed landscape" involves the use of framing devices to draw the viewer's attention to a distant view or one at a different eye level so that it becomes visually incorporated into the garden.

Above: *The most crystalline of designs, the dry garden at the Zen Mountain Monastery in New York directs the viewer's eye into the heart of the symbolic landscape. The patterns of raked gravel may suggest the flow and energy of water or, conversely, stasis and calm.*

The teahouse garden, too, presents a viewer with a symbolic journey. Traditionally called the *roji* or "dewy path," it prepared a celebrant for the tea ritual by leading him out of the world, full of distractions, into sacred space. Legend has it that the plant that yielded tea sprang from the eyelids of the Bodhidharma, founder of Zen, who plucked them off so that he could stay fully awake during his nine-year meditation. Tea has a long medicinal history, and it seems likely that the tea ceremony had its roots in the habit of monks who drank tea to stay alert during long periods of meditation, evolving into a stylized ritual to honor Bodhidharma.

The design of the tea garden works to make the celebrant fully conscious and aware of ordinary acts, among them walking and drinking. The demarcation between the outside world and the tea garden can be either symbolic or literal; sometimes the celebrant passes through a gate or into an outer courtyard before walking the "dewy path." The design of the path—sometimes circuitous and always marked by stepping stones placed in a pattern—forces the celebrant to slow down and make his walking mindful. Both the plantings—lichens, moss, and ferns among them—and the building itself are deliberately rustic and weathered, and offer no visual distractions. Lanterns, once used as

Above left: *In the Zen garden, a few carefully chosen elements resound with greater meaning. Here, carefully patterned rocks symbolize flowing water; changelessness is articulated in a rock; illumination captured in the stone lantern; and purification captured in the stone basin.*

Above: *A stone guardian marks sacred space in the Korean Ambassador's garden, designed by Jeff Lee, in Washington, D.C.*

votive offerings in both Shinto shrines and Buddhist temples are incorporated into the garden to light the path, as are stone basins, used for ritual purification before the celebrant enters the teahouse, and a well yielding water for brewing the tea. The degree to which the garden is part of a symbolic preparation for ritual is made clear by the traditional entrance to the teahouse itself which is deliberately small, requiring the celebrant to bend over or symbolically humble himself before entering, stripping another layer of worldliness in the process.

As the tea ceremony increased in social importance in the fifteenth and sixteenth centuries, the symbolic design vocabulary associated with the *rijo*—the stepping stones, the lantern, and the water basin— were incorporated into small inner courtyard gardens. While these gardens were never meant to be walked in and in fact bear no connection to the tea ceremony, they are full-scale gardens that, like the other Japanese gardens, suggest the larger landscape, the universal, beyond the specifics in a small space. Pared-down, artful groupings of balanced elements, these courtyard gardens provided a model that can easily be adapted for a garden sanctuary in either the countryside or in the city.

These gardens of spirit create a very specific relationship between the viewer or visitor and the garden itself. As Dennis Piermont, a landscape designer of many Japanese gardens and a partner in New York City's LANDGARDEN, notes, "the viewer completes the garden, bringing to it the dimension the garden itself does not possess." The relationship between the gardener and the garden takes on a different dimension, too, in these gardens; here, Piermont notes, "the designer idealizes nature, strips it down to its essence, in order to reveal the reality

Above left: *The smallest of water features adds detail and energy to this private garden.*

Above: *In this garden, an epiphany of in and yo is captured in the flow of water over rock.*

of nature." What in the West is called nature and is associated with the burgeoning life force expressed in plants and flowers takes on an entirely different form and interpretation in these Eastern sacred spaces. The wild, the unkempt, the random—all associated with the Western idea of nature—have no place in these sanctuaries. Maggie Oster, author of *Reflections of the Spirit: Japanese Gardens in America*, tells the story of an early twentieth-century American, Florence du Cane, who, visiting an otherwise apparently immaculate monastery garden, was surprised by what she took to be the "litter" of pine needles strewn about. Only when she looked closely did she realize that each pine needle had been deliberately placed to represent

the flow of water; the pattern of needles actually "eddied" as real water would when interrupted by a stone. The distinction we in the West would make between "aesthetic" and "spiritual," Maggie notes, is not part of the Japanese tradition; every element in the garden has spiritual significance even as it has aesthetic value.

Just as there is no distinction between the aesthetic and the spiritual, Zen and the Zen garden deny the parallel distinction between the spiritual and the mundane. Because the ordinary task was believed to yield ultimate enlightenment, part of the discipline in a Zen monastery entailed bringing mindfulness and perfection to each and every task, no matter humble or lowly.

Every monk worked and, to emphasize the importance of the ordinary, the wisest of the monks performed the most menial and tedious of tasks, while the novices were assigned the lightest of duties. In the Zen tradition pruning and maintenance—the removal of dead leaves, broken or damaged

Above far left: *Because of its fleeting beauty, the cherry blossom is both an image of earthly bliss and prosperity as well as an emblem of the end which awaits us all.*

Above center: *The exquisite morning glory* (Ipomoea 'Heavenly Blue') *is prized both for its beauty and its evanescence.*

Above: *The lotus is the supreme emblem of spiritual emergence.*

branches, and other material—are not only a part of the symbolism of the garden (contributing to its permanence and its harmony) and its aesthetic (the refinement of its details to an ideal), but of its spiritual discipline. In a dry garden the raking of gravel into patterns to suggest the flow of water and the removal of debris once again fulfill symbolic, aesthetic, and spiritual aims. The interconnection of the spiritual and the aesthetic, as well as of the spiritual and the mundane, is attested to in another famous anecdote, again involving the famous master Rikyu: Rikyu was teaching his son to clean the tea garden and, as his father instructed, the boy did, picking out all the dead leaves, carefully tending every fern leaf, removing every cobweb and, finally, sprinkling every rock and bit of moss with water. The master came to survey his son's work and pronounced it unfinished, so the boy began anew, sweeping the ground and the moss with a twig broom, wiping down each leaf, and sprinkling the garden with water. Rikyu looked at the garden again and shook his head, and the boy protested, saying he had done everything asked, not once but many times. Without saying a word, Rikyu reached and shook the branch of a small maple tree. A cascade of red leaves settled

on the moss, and Rikyu pronounced the garden finished.

Because they depend on the arrangement of a few carefully chosen elements, these sacred spaces, even the stroll garden, can be adapted as home sanctuaries, no matter how large or small. The lessons taught by the these traditions of landscape design are especially valuable, since they remind us of the interconnection of all things, and permit us to locate ourselves in the landscape of our gardens.

Above: *Nestled under a tree, surrounded by fallen leaves and other evidence of the natural cycle, this exquisite statue of the Buddha invites the viewer to contemplate sacred space.*

THE *Gaia* GARDEN

The old men say

the earth

only

endures

you spoke

truly you are right.

Sioux, "The Earth Only Endures"

 The sacred spaces we have called Gaia's gardens take their name from the Greek goddess *Ge* or Rhea, the mother of Zeus's Olympian pantheon and the symbol of the prepatriarchal order. These are all sanctuaries that honor the earth as Mother; in some, the garden becomes a place to celebrate the divine feminine in nature. All over the world, in different cultures, humanity has understood the earth to be feminine, the womb from which all life emerges. These earth-honoring gardens draw on different spiritual traditions but each of them is founded in the understanding of the earth as inherently sacred, whole unto itself, and a living organism. In these

natural landscape, remembering that the word "inform" refers both to knowledge and inspiration. In these gardens, the cultivation of sacred space draws on knowledge and spirit in equal parts.

When we give up the "my" and the "mine" in the Gaia garden, seeing the earth as a living legacy supplants the understanding of the earth as a resource to be plundered. Through gardening we increase our awareness of the true costs of "progress" in the last century, the measurable decline in the planet's diverse patterns of life among them. Choosing plants for the Gaia garden has us look in directions other than the usual offerings at the local nursery. We turn to heirloom gardening—retrieving and growing varieties of flowers, fruits, and vegetables that existed before twentieth-century advances in hybridization—and seed saving—growing from heirloom seeds and then harvesting new seeds at the end of the growing season—to add a new dimension to gardening for the spirit. Growing heirlooms and seed-saving permit us to make an active commitment to preserving biodiversity in our own backyards at a time when the entire planet's heritage of genetic diversity is threatened. Seed-saving puts us, as Tessa Gowans of the Abundant Life Seed Foundation notes, "directly into the whole process and cycle of nature, from beginning to ending to beginning again." In addition to integrating the gardener into the process of life and making a part of the garden truly self-sustaining, seed-saving has other emotional and spiritual benefits as well. Tessa notes that an interest in seed-saving usually begins with a familial connection, when people either find seeds left to them by a family member or are taught the process; Tessa was her grandmother's apprentice and, when she gardens with the seeds of plants that were first sown two generations ago, she actively preserves her own past as well as that of the earth. By taking responsibility for reclaiming the gardening past—restoring our literal roots—we take on the spiritual wisdom of our ancestral elders, while assuring a continuous legacy for the

sanctuaries we give up the possessives of everyday life, the "my" and "mine," and we bring the inclusiveness of "our" to bear on the entire physical world to nurture our spirits. Here our active and informed participation in the continuing health of the earth and the sustenance of its extraordinary variety becomes a spiritual exercise not only for the individual but for the family and community, for this generation and the next. The adjectives "active" and "informed" describe the common thread that links all of these different sanctuaries. We become "active" by taking responsibility for our immediate surroundings, which includes stewardship and preservation of the garden's ecology. We are "informed" by close observation of the

Above: *The seedheads of sunflowers provide a microcosmic view of how the planet as a whole works: nature renewing itself.*

Previous pages: *In sculptor Audrey Flack's garden, a nineteenth-century statue of an angel presides over its growth.*

generations of gardeners who follow us. We become teachers to a new generation as we learn. Sharing and trading seeds from our gardens with other gardeners has the added advantage, too, of forging a link to a community of likeminded individuals through gardening.

Then, too, as in any garden, there are lessons of spirit to be learned from the act of gardening itself. Tessa tells the story of one of her own favorite seeds, the Cherokee corn field bean, a vital part of Cherokee tribal tradition. Traditionally these seeds represent what Tessa calls an "insurance mix" to ensure a bountiful harvest: even when planted all at once, the beans will not only come up at different times but will thrive under very different conditions, some flourishing in dry soil and others in wet. The mix is visually diverse: the beans that grow from the seeds are different colors—some are even striped rather than solid—and yield flowers of different colors, ranging from reds to lavenders to whites. Some gardeners, Tessa reports, have been tempted by a vision of uniformity and have tried to harvest and save specific seeds deliberately, only to end up with a failed crop. The message, she says laughingly, is "Don't mess!"; the balance in the mix is apparently a necessary one. The spiritual message about the unseen web of relationship is even more profound.

In this garden, we also look to wildflower gardening to connect us to the spirit of the Earth Mother. Different criteria govern the creation of a wildflower garden; we need to familiarize ourselves with the topography of the area in which we live, and study native plants in the wild. By choosing native plants and paying close attention to light and soil conditions, we bring a different kind of reciprocity to our relationship to Mother Earth. Keep in mind that wildflower gardening is still an act of cultivation; respect the earth and don't cull plants from the wild to incorporate into your garden. Remember, too, that, in most states, specific wildflowers—some on the verge of extinction because of changes to their native

That our earth mother
May wear a fourfold green robe,
Full of moss,
Full of flowers,
Full of pollen,
That the land may be thus
I have made you into living beings.

Zuni "Prayer"

Above: *The burgeoning life force is everywhere evident in the garden; here, narcissus emerges from the bulb.*

115

habitat or the introduction of non-native competitive plants—are protected by law.

Planting wildflowers, too, is an act of restoration. Neil Diboll of Prairie Nursery in Westfield, Wisconsin, rightly calls the interest in native plants a "gradual but significant leap in North American consciousness," as people abandon the view of the natural landscape as a resource to be exploited and discover instead the value of becoming a 'steward' of the land. (He points out that "it is only recently that we as a culture have come to place an economic value on natural ecosystems. As natural landscapes and open spaces become increasingly rare, their 'marginal value' increases with their rarity." He adds that, "in an increasingly crowded, impersonal and detached world, the spiritual renewal provided by unspoiled landscapes becomes a valuable and even priceless asset.") Using native plants in the garden, Neil notes, transcends the idea of the garden as a reflection of self: "When we incorporate native plants, we can feel tangible satisfaction because we are re-clothing earth with diverse plant communities." A garden full of native plants, he says, can change a person's very relationship with the earth.

While heirloom and wildflower gardening teach us valuable lessons about the nature of stewardship in the new millennium, the legacy of the Native Americans has much to tell us about how our own spiritual and physical lives are connected to the earth on which we live. Barrie Kavasch, horticulturist and Native American expert, reminds us that the spiritual teachers of the Native Americans knew to "read" the earth and to listen to "what the plants have to tell us." As Barrie explains it, because Native Americans understood the relationship between humanity and earth as fully reciprocal—expressed in gestures of thankfulness when plants were harvested or animals slain—they also knew that certain obvious changes in plant populations had a prophetic quality, "the Creator's and Mother Earth's way of showing what would be needed by the tribe in the future." Even though Native Americans managed their wild resources—taking the roots and seeds of healing plants with them as they moved to reestablish them in new surroundings—they also were attentive to changes in the landscape, understanding the proliferation of certain plants as signals of the future. The growth and adaptation of native plants in the Gaia garden teaches us about the larger patterns of growth on the planet. In the medicine wheel garden Barrie has designed for The Institute of American Indian Studies (see page 71 for a fuller description), the plant colonies of native healing plants are always changing, a living lesson in growth and companionship. (Yarrow, Barrie points out, is traditionally considered an herb of strength for the healing arts of many cultures, including those of the Native Americans; in the medicine wheel garden, plants around yarrow show enhanced growth.) In Barrie's personal sacred space, a garden in a country setting on the East Coast, she has planted a native creeper, trumpet vine, underneath the most mature of her black walnut trees. Although black walnuts are usually cited as extremely poor companions for other plants (because of the chemicals their roots exude); in Barrie's space this is a marriage made in heaven: The vine has wound itself around the tree in a veritable embrace, creating what Barrie calls a "cathedral" for hummingbirds who come to sup on the trumpets.

Honoring the earth as Mother also invites us to look outside the precincts of our gardens. Barrie takes meditative walks along the narrow animal trails that crisscross her meadows and lawns, which show, in her words, "the regular comings and goings of deer, coyotes, fox, rabbits, wild turkeys, and occasional weasels and minks," imbuing her property "with their urgencies and energies" and deepening her own "sense of loving the land." She comments, "I feel a close restorative gratefulness on these paths, since the paths of the woodland creatures reassure me that the web of life is secure in my region. These are the networks of livelihood that help to weave our organic commitments, while assuring that our gardens will be the local salad bar."

Environmental stewardship can also entail restoring the web of life, as it has in Kansas City, Missouri, on the

Opposite: *At the San Francisco Zen Center's Green Gulch Farm (also known as Green Dragon Temple) in Marin County, California, heirloom flowers are harvested for cutting, bringing the sacred space of outdoors inside.*

Above right: *In this garden designed by Chris Jacobson, part of the effort was to recycle as much of the existing garden as possible, limiting the amout of debris that needed to be carted off. Trees were salvaged, as were concrete, stones, and pottery shards, and made a part of the refurbished landscape. Here, a runnel leads to a pond.*

grounds of Abiding Peace Lutheran Church, where four acres of lawn have been transformed to create an outdoor sanctuary for worshipers, members of the larger community, and wildlife. On what was once prairie flatlands, the church stands amid buildings, a shopping center, and a K-Mart; up until eight years ago the treeless property was nothing more than flat lawn, with a swampy area behind the main building. Mary Gerken, a parishioner who has long been personally and professionally involved with ecology (she works for the Environmental Protection Agency), enlisted the help of the aptly named Jan Vinyard from Longview Gardens to develop a new landscape design for the church as part of a "creation-awareness ministry." Native plants were chosen both because they

were low maintenance and provided the habitat necessary to the wildlife Mary hoped to attract to the grounds. The perimeter of the property is marked by a trail of wood chips, enjoyed both as a meditation path—there are signs with Bible verses for contemplation throughout the landscape—and a nature walk. The trail is planted with a variety of trees and bushes, among them filberts, honeysuckle, persimmon, Kentucky coffee trees, elderberries, and apple and pear trees. Within the boundaries of the property are 17 community garden plots, one of which is used as a therapeutic tool by a local mental facility; a meditation garden that includes a butterfly area, planted with cardinal-flowers, coneflowers, rose of Sharon, and buddleia; a

prairie restoration area planted with native grasses and wildflowers; and a berry patch with a cherry tree and currants, blackberries, gooseberries, and strawberries. The design also includes two water features specially designed for birds and other creatures: a small pond with water lilies and other aquatic plants and a "giant bird bath," a shallow area at the edge of the prairie area encircled by cattails and native irises. The backyard meditation garden— which Mary describes as "a quiet place where you meet God and see evidence of His presence"—has a "strawberry" lawn, and the fruits themselves have been made into jam to share with visitors. Grapevines grow in both a meditation garden and an arbor which has become a place to hold ser-

vices. While the grapes harvested yield home-grown communion wine, the vines themselves—and the tending of them—put into literal form one of the most potent metaphors of Scripture. Mary points out that all the references to "I am the vine and you are the branches" take on different meaning when "you've had to prune the vines yourself, since they grow about 15 feet a year!" The quiet of this garden is enhanced by the presence of a weeping willow, which

Above, from left to right: *Organic vegetable beds at the Rudolf Steiner Fellowship Foundation in New York; an organic vegetable garden with a meandering path; compost covered in rose petals; an organic vegetable, herb, and flower garden in the home of artists Missy and Tommy Simpson.*

thrives in the once-swampy ground. This lovely sanctuary for both the congregation and the community has also become one for wildlife; along with butterflies, rabbits, and squirrels, a pair of mockingbirds feeds off the berry patch, while a robin calls the grape arbor home. And the sight of a family of killdeer nesting on the nature trail has become a harbinger of spring for one and all.

There are many different ways of recovering our sense of the Earth Mother. The Gaia garden—whether it takes the form of the Native American medicine wheel, a simple vegetable garden, a bed of native plants, or a meadow filled with prairie grasses and wildflowers— can become a place where we

connect to earth by observing the divine in the small details. Include a seating area in the Gaia garden so that you, friends, and family can sit and actually watch the changes in plants and trees week by week, month by month, and learn from them. Allow your eyes and spirit to see what they normally don't take the time to observe by writing in a journal or sketching the plants in the garden, and taking in the spectrum of life at different times of the day.

A garden sanctuary which honors the earth can take on many forms. Painter and sculptor Audrey Flack's garden on Long Island, on a property that was once the site of Native American healing rites, honors the feminine with a garden

dominated by two statues, a French nineteenth-century sculpture of an angel who acts as the "guardian" of the space and a Native American goddess, sculpted by Audrey herself, which celebrates the Earth Mother. The different garden areas over which they preside, separated by an alleé, articulate the energy and spirit of the feminine and earth. English landscape designer and plantswoman Pamela Woods, who specializes in sacred gardens, is creating a sacred space for a client that honors the ancient feminine force associated with earth. Once an English "kitchen" garden some 200 feet square—one that supplied the home with herbs and vegetables— Pamela's newly designed Goddess garden now makes an old well its

119

focal point since, for millennia, the divine feminine has always been closely associated with the depths of the waters. Radiating paths and geometric forms, executed in different colors of cobblestones, emanate from the well; around the well itself is the form of a five-petaled rose, an ancient symbol of the sacred and the feminine, as well as universal love in the Tarot. This garden in Hampshire is in the midst of an old woodland area filled with English native plants such as oak and beech trees, holly and laurel, dog's mercury, bluebells, and ground elder, and Pamela has deliberately left an area of wilderness in this cultivated space for those plants that reflect the larger landscape outside of the garden's walls. In adddition Pamela's design incorporates distinct garden areas which reflect different aspects of the divine feminine. When the

garden is complete, a winding path will lead from the hot tub to an area associated with the element fire planted with bronze-leaved plants such as New Zealand flax; the fire that is love will be celebrated visually with a statue of Venus surrounded by red climbing roses. In another area of the garden, close to the house, Pamela will create a "moon" garden, representing that aspect of the feminine traditionally connected to the lunar cycles; here she will plant white and silver-leaved plants to reflect the light of the moon. Some, like santolina, will be clipped into globes, a reflection of the heavenly body on the ground. Because this space honors Mother Earth, Pamela has made the vegetable garden—normally tucked out of view to the side of the house in English landscaping—an integral part of the sacred space. When she chose plantings for this garden, as she has for the other sacred spaces she's designed, Pamela worked intuitively; using her training as a botanist, she observed what grew naturally in the landscape and then, after studying light and soil conditions, added plants that would thrive in the environment.

Finally, because the Gaia garden celebrates the earth as a community, use this sanctuary to celebrate the boun-

Left: *The native coneflower (Echinacea purpurea)—both beautiful and an important medicinal—becomes a living metaphor for the gifts of Mother Earth.*

Opposite top: *The Medicine Wheel garden at the Institute for American Indian Studies is both a place to honor the earth and earth-honoring traditions. For more on this garden, please see page 71.*

Opposite bottom: *A second cast of sculptor Audrey Flack's own work, Quewe Pehelle graces her spiritual garden. The statue, whose name in Native American means "stream that flows from beneath the pines," was created for Lebanon Valley College in Pennsylvania and commemorates the spirit of the land and its original inhabitants who were slaughtered. The statue symbolizes the return of the land to those who first lived on it.*

ties of the earth with friends, family, and community. Exchange saved seeds with a friend or neighbor. Think of the garden as an opportunity to teach your children about the spirit of the earth; growing a birdhouse gourd, drying it, and then hanging it the following year, for example, is a perfect way to teach them about the web of life in the garden. Small children, all those past the point of putting things in their mouths, can participate in seed-saving: Try sunflowers, cleome, black-eyed Susans, and impatiens. The latter, writer Leslie Garisto reports, are a particular favorite of her seven-year-old daughter because of the pop of the seed capsule when it is touched! Even planting a heart- or circle-shaped bed of radishes—which can easily be grown from seed and then harvested by small hands—is a testament to the wonder and spirit that are part of the fabric of the Earth Mother's "green robe."

THE *Aromatherapy* GARDEN

Into my face a miracle

Of orchard-breath, and with the smell —

I know not how such things can be! —

I breathed my soul back into me.

Edna St. Vincent Millay

 Humanity has long known that fragrances can calm our feelings or arouse them; it is said that Cleopatra scented the sails of her already sweet-smelling cedarwood barge before she set off to meet Mark Antony, and that she bedded him in a room with a deep litter of rose petals. For thousands of years, human beings have used scent for religious purposes: The burning of incense, resins, grasses, and herbs heightens the awareness of participants in ritual, while scented oils and fragrant smoke render objects such as ritual tools, statuary, and altars holy in spiritual traditions all over the world. From ancient times forward, floral fragrance, too, symbolized the intangible spirit, perhaps because perfume lingers in the air even after its source is no longer present; thus flowers play a part in burial and other ceremonies in cultures the world over. Scent has long been thought to heal and revive both body and spirit, and what we now call aromatherapy has ancient roots.

This garden is a special kind of sanctuary, dedicated to awakening our spirit through scent. It is, by its very nature, a garden of variety, meant to stimulate and teach us about the connection between body and soul. It is a sensuous garden that invites us to experience pleasure. Scent's ability to heighten or transform our feelings and, according to some, our physical well-being has garnered acknowledgment and acceptance with the increasing popularity of aromatherapy in contemporary times. The term "aromatherapy" is an invention of the twentieth century, coined by a French chemist, René Gatefossé, in the 1930s. Although popularly the word "aromatherapy" is now used very broadly—referring to scented candles, bath oils, even pillows filled

Above: *In a corner of a garden, the addition of a simple bench, near plantings of thyme and lavender, yields a place where scent can heal.*

Previous pages: *In aromatherapist Jeanne Rose's garden, a deliberately crooked path (since, as she says, the devil hates one) winds its way through plantings of roses, wormwood, and wisteria.*

Left: *The lush scents of oranges and verbena perfume the air and hearten the soul at Mount Calvary in California.*

with aromatic materials—technically aromatherapy is a form of holistic healing that involves inhaling or applying essential herbal oils. These essential oils, a mixture of natural chemical compounds, are the basis for scent in a plant's leaves or flowers. The oils are obtained from plant material through a variety of methods, including extraction, enfleurage, expression, and distillation. Highly concentrated and not inert (they not only change when isolated but when they come into contact with the body), essential oils have been touted as beneficial to mental health and physical well-being. Users, though, should recognize that they are also potentially dangerous, allergenic, and contraindicated for pregnant women as well as others with specific medical conditions. Some essential oils should not be used at all without the advice of a medical practitioner; all esssential oils must be handled and used with safety in mind. Keep in mind, too, that rigorous scientific investigation has not validated most of the specific claims for aromatherapy made by its practitioners.

The act of planning and working in a garden dedicated to scent is a journey away from fragmentation, toward wholeness and engagement. This is a spiritual garden that helps us understand the limitations of the either/ors we've been taught—the opposing choices of mind or body, intellect or emotion, material or spiritual—and lets us feel the power of "and" by focusing our attention on a single sense. Smell, the most primitive and least understood of our senses, is also the most undervalued. Most of us, if asked, would rank our sense of smell far below the others in its importance to living our life fully. Sight surely would rank first, then hearing or touch, then taste, or perhaps these four grouped together in importance; last would come what Helen Keller—who was deprived of her sight and hearing—called the "fallen angel": smell. The darkness of blindness, the impenetrable quiet of deafness, the tomb of unfeeling, even the loss of the pleasure of food are much more readily imagined than the losses presented by a scent-

less world. We may not fully appreciate our sense of smell because we no longer perceive ourselves to depend on it for our basic needs and survival as our ancient ancestors did. Or perhaps, because our ability to describe or capture the essence of fragrance in language is so incredibly limited, we mistakenly assume that smell itself is of limited value. No dictionary contains the verbal arsenal we need to describe the fragrance of living sap in a twig or the scent of a specific flower. Because as a culture we seem dedicated to removing as much "natural" scent from our bodies and our immediate environment as possible, we tend to be conscious of this specific sense only in the presence of attractive or repellent odors or on those occasions when, temporarily deprived of our sense of smell, we can't taste what we eat.

But in fact, we engage our sense of smell throughout our lives, from the first to the last breath we take. In *A Natural History of the Senses*, Diane Ackerman notes that as we inhale and exhale, air passes over our olfactory sites;

we breathe 23,000 times a day, and move over 400 cubic feet of air around us. Science has shown that human babies recognize their mothers not simply by the sounds of their voices heard in utero but by their smell. If spiritual awareness is sentience, then this garden offers us a unique opportunity to reawaken this important sense and make ourselves fully conscious. That awareness comes not only from the scents of the plants, the earth beneath our knees, and the air above our heads but from the smell of our skin and the fragrances left by plant materials on our hands. As we garden, our sense of smell integrates us into the landscape.

Becoming aware of the variety of scents in the natural world—in the soil, bark, seed, leaf, flower—lets us inhale the details our eyes miss. In this sanctuary we let one sense enrich the perceptions of the other four. Close your eyes as you dig in the earth right after a heavy rain and your fingers and your nose will "see" what your eyes cannot: the thick, clingy clods of the soil and its heavy, almost musky

scent. Eyes open, the pungency of anise hyssop (*Agastache foeniculum*), so called for the licorelike scent of its leaves, is given definition by the sight of its beautiful mauve-purple flowers. We touch the silver-green leaves of Russian sage (*Perovskia atriplicifolia*) with our fingers or brush against them with our legs and, as we touch, we release a bouquet of scents. With our eyes closed, we take in the scent of the ornamental tobacco (*Nicotiana* sp.), whose strong fragrance belies its delicacy of form.

In the aromatherapy garden, the hardest part of planning is choosing what to plant, given the enormous variety of scents and the different experiences each of these scents offers. While most flowering plants and shrubs need full sun to flourish, certain shade plants—some hostas (particularly cultivars of *Hosta plantaginea* such as 'Sweet Susan'), a variety of meadowsweet called queen of the meadow (*Filipendula ulmaria*), and *Astilbe rosea* 'Peach Blossom'— will add both fragrance and texture to the garden. Using scent as the basis for the garden permits you to create a landscape based on contrasts, combining such sweet-smelling plants as lemon verbena (*Aloysia triphylla*), cottage pink (*Dianthus plumarius*), and sweet rocket (*Hesperis matronalis*) with pungent ones, such as members of the onion family (*Allium* sp). Experiment with scented plants that recall taste: the curry plant (*Helichrysum petiolatum*) or the various mints (*Mentha* sp.); the aptly named apple mint (*Mentha suaveolens*) or chocolate mint (*M.* x *piperita* 'Chocolate'). Scent can permeate all levels of this sacred space, above our heads, at our hands, and below our feet. Plant a variety of climbing rose or jasmine (*Jasminum* sp.) along a trellis or a fence for airborne scent; pine-scented thyme

Above: *A bower of roses creates a special kind of sacred space, filled with fragrance and beauty.*

Opposite far right: *A path of chamomile, its scent released by the vistor's footfalls, leads to a small fountain in this garden of spirit.*

Opposite right: *A small garden filled with varieties of thyme.*

(*Thymus caespititius*), Corsican mint (*Mentha requienii*), or chamomile (*Chamaemelum nobile*) which gives off an apple scent can be planted as a fragrant carpet.

Planting different varieties of a single aromatic herb permits us to experience the amazing diversity of the natural world through our sense of smell. The herb thyme (*Thymus*) has always been associated with increased sensation; it was, in times past, reputed to endow courage, heighten sexual desire, and enable a person to see the normally invisible sprites and fairies in the garden. Thyme's fragrance has its own, understated glory; Rudyard Kipling wrote of the "wind-bit thyme that smells like dawn in Paradise." Common thyme (*T. vulgaris*) is a bushy shrub, with green-gray leaves and tiny white to lilac flowers; it has a fresh "green" scent, familiar to cooks. Camphor thyme (*T. camphoratus*), on the other hand, smells just as its name would suggest, has dark green leaves, and no flowers. Caraway thyme (*T. herba-barona*), too, smells like its common namesake and has lavender flowers and dark, shiny green leaves; another variety, *T. herba-barona* 'Nutmeg', this one with pink flowers and fatter stalks, has an even spicier scent. Lemon thyme (*T. x citriodorus*), with its glossy green leaves, has both a lemon smell and

taste. A carpet of woolly thyme (*T. pseudolanuginosis*) has a slightly musky, green scent and a distinct texture because of its dense, hairy leaves. A small garden bed planted with some or all of these varieties of thyme presents a wonderful opportunity for awakening the senses.

Even plants traditionally associated with a single, readily identifiable scent can surprise us with the amazing subtlety of their differences. Lavender (*Lavandula angustifolia*), perhaps the most exquisite of all floral scents, has, for thousands of years, comforted the heart and cleansed the soul with its sweet smell. (Its name comes from

127

the Latin, meaning "to wash," for both the Greeks and Romans scented their bathwater with it.) Yet even lavender offers a rainbow of scents along with subtle shadings of color: 'Munstead' lavender has lovely deep purple flowers, silvery green leaves, and a lush clear scent, while 'Hidcote' lavender releases its pure, intense fragrance if you brush against it. French Lavender (*L. stoechas*) smells like rosemary and has velvety whitish leaves and dark purple flowers. And then, of course,

there are the varieties of the rose—a banquet table piled high with possibilities in terms of fragrance, color, texture, and form. Horticulturist and garden designer Jaen Treesinger remembers her visit to the splendid 45-year-old sanctuary of a woman who has since become a friend. This extraordinary garden of old-fashioned roses—over 1,000 different varieties—was, quite literally, intoxicating to behold; Jaen remembers the euphoria induced by the scents and sights, imbuing her with an energy

she felt for days and days. As a professional with over 20 years of experience, Jaen notes that fragrance is an important element in the design of any garden; scent can, in her words, "create emotion in the garden setting, as well as drawing in wildlife," and she works with clients to determine their specific emotional connections to fragrance.

We come into this sanctuary to connect with our inner selves through scent. Because scent has the ability to elicit memory, remembered scents in nature permit us to reconnect to different moments in our lives. Often our memories of scent are drawn from our childhood experiences; Linda, an avid gardener, has

Above: *This exquisite aromatherapy garden is a special kind of sanctuary, brimful of color and scent, a haven full of light and life. Its path leads us on a journey of the senses, letting us breath deep and free our souls. Among the plantings are heliotrope, salvia, tobacco plant* (Nicotiana alata), *Russian sage* (Perovskia atriplicifolia), *oregano* (Origanum vulgare), *and purple coneflower* (Echinacea purpurea).

planted lavender in her garden, a scent she associates with her grandmother whose clothing always smelled faintly of the lavender potpourri she kept in her drawers. Each summer when the lavender is in full bloom, Linda feels her memories of her grandmother, who was an important role model and mentor, become more immediate and accessible. In this spiritual garden we let memory become an active wellspring for the soul. Yet fragrance does more than connect us to the past. Because scents in the garden can be intense, overshadowing other sensations, they permit us to experience the present with terrific immediacy. Each different season has its own particular

fragrance, a combination of scents released by all the living elements of the garden—the soil, the trees, the flowers. The scent of just-mown grass, after the hiatus of winter, captures early spring in fragrance, while the sweet, almost sticky intensity of mid-summer perfumes are no less vivid than the heat of the sun on your skin. The smell of fallen leaves, neither fully fresh nor musty, captures one essence of autumn, while the slightly acrid "green" scent of the twig snapped off in a winter storm confirms the life that sleeps below the surface.

The soul work of this garden remains very much connected to the body. Experience this sanctuary not

only on a bright sunny day but after a rain or in the evening to really understand the many layers of fragrance in the garden, and remember that, in Rabindranath Tagore's words, "the smell of the wet earth rises like a great chant of praise."

Because of the fragile and fleeting nature of scent, fragrance preaches sermons about the ephemeral and homilies about change and the final passing of time.

From left to right: French lavender (Lavendula stoechis); pineapple shrub (Calycanthus floridus); garlic in flower (Allium sativum); and the smell of earth: the blended scents of mushrooms, fallen pine needles, and leaves.

THE *Feng Shui* GARDEN

Thus it is that the Tao produces all things,

nourishes them, brings them to their full growth,

nurses them, completes them, matures them,

maintains them, and shelters them.

Attributed to Lao Tzu

As more of us in the West become conscious of the spiritual and other costs of our separation from nature, interest in the ancient Chinese art of feng shui and its application to both the home and the garden has grown. In contrast to Western practice, where homes and buildings are designed without any specific orientation to the natural landscape—save, perhaps, to take advantage of a view or to gain privacy—the Chinese have, for roughly 3,000 years, acknowledged the direct relationships among the landscape, the structures built and developed on it, and the prosperity of the people who live in them. Feng shui—which literally means "wind and water"—is an art specifically concerned with how the energy of the natural surroundings affects human well-being, aspirations, and achievements. The principles of feng shui can be used to make an existing garden more harmonious or to enrich the design and symbolism of many of the spiritual gardens described in these pages. Since feng shui draws on the meaning and influence of the four cardinal directions as well as the points in between them, it can also be used to help site any spiritual garden, whether its focus is healing, tranquillity or meditation, or earth-honoring, as well as help you decide where to place a water feature or statue.

Feng shui grew out of and remains intimately connected to Taoism, which is both a religion and a philosophy based on the balance and patterns inherent in nature. "Tao" means both principle and process, as well as path or road; the word "process" is important to feng shui since the discipline envisions a world that is made up of the continuous interaction among humanity, nature, and the forces at work in all things, yin and yang. (See also "Gardening for the Soul," page 8.) From this point of view, using a pesticide that kills both pests and beneficial insects is not simply bad stewardship; it is also bad feng shui since the balance of yin and yang in the soil has been destroyed. As Mark Leuchten, a feng shui landscape designer remarks, "Feng shui requires that we see the garden and gardening holistically. In ancient China cosmology was understood as a triad made up of heaven, earth, and humanity. In the feng shui garden, we acknowledge the influence of the person on the garden as well as the influence of the garden on the person." Applying the principles of feng shui in the garden leads us to work to restore the balance in nature.

The most important tenet of feng shui is *chi*, sometimes called "the Dragon's breath" the energy of the life force, the flow of which is affected by living creatures, topographical features, and inanimate objects such as buildings and fences. Chi itself is manifested in the five elements that make up all things—fire, water, wood, metal, and earth—and that constantly interact; and can relate in either creative or destructive cycles. The soft, sometimes meandering edges and curves of nature allow the best flow of chi; in contrast, certain elements—straight lines, triangular forms, sharp corners—can make chi flow too quickly. Conversely, narrow openings and other impediments to chi flow can make it stagnate. Simply put, where there is a harmonious flow of chi, there is spiritual and physical health and abundance, and good feng shui; where chi is stagnant or "cutting"—forced by

Left: *In this feng shui garden, the flow of water symbolizes energy and fluidity, while the seasonal irises testify to the constantly changing nature of time.*

Previous pages: *The Moon Gate at the Chinese Scholar's Garden at the Staten Island Botanical Garden.*

angles and corners—or where the elements are in a destructive cycle, spiritual and physical well-being and good feng shui are absent. As a part of the natural landscape the feng shui of the garden can be adjusted and maximized to benefit the spiritual and material lives of those who use and enjoy it. As Jami Lin, a feng shui expert, notes, "Spirit is a mani-

Above: *The beautiful water feature in Jami Lin's garden increases chi and strengthens the area devoted to career and journey.*

Right: *In the same garden, the pergola is hung with sculptures that permit the energy to flow evenly, while the guardians protect the entrance.*

festation of chi, and simply looking at the shimmer dance of leaves in the garden makes us aware of the chi moving around us, and so reconnects us to spirit."

Contemporary feng shui is practiced according to the tenets of traditional schools as well as new variations upon them, such as "intuitive" feng shui. The oldest school, that of the Land Form, developed out of ancestral worship in the mountainous region of southern China. The proper burial of an ancestor, in an auspicious place where chi flowed, would, it was thought, secure the fortunes of succeeding generations, just as the auspicious location of a home would

further the fortunes of those who lived within it. Land Form feng shui concerns itself with the relationship and shapes of the landscape elements: hills, mountains, and bodies of water. Different shapes are associated with colors, sacred animals, and the cardinal directions: the green dragon in the east, the white tiger in the west, the black tortoise in the north, and the red phoenix in the south. According to the Land Form school, ideally a home or garden should face south and have a high hill or mountain for protection in the back or north, and two lower hills on either side, signifying nurturance. On a literal level this configuration—sometimes referred to as "armchair"—protects the home from winds and buffeting by the elements and as provides security. On a

symbolic level it means that the house is protected by its animal guardians: the tortoise symbolizes longevity, while the pairing of the dragon—symbol of prosperity and yang in nature—with the protector tiger—yin in nature— yields harmony and balance. In a contemporary setting lacking the hills and mountains of China, a stand of tall trees could stand for the turtle, while the green dragon and white tiger could be the homes of neighbors.

A second system of feng shui, the Compass school, developed in the northern plains of China, where there was little topography to guide the feng shui master as he had been in the south. Different tools were used to assess a site, among them the eight trigrams of the I Ching, the eight-sided figure called the *bagua* (sometimes known as the *pa kua*), a *Lo Shu* or magic square, and a complicated compass (the *Luo pan*) aligned with both the cardinal points and the sun, moon, and stars. More recently a third school of feng shui, one with a more spiritual emphasis, called the Black Hat Sect was developed by Professor Lin Yun in the United States, which uses the bagua as well as intuition.

The bagua helps explain how the various aspects of feng shui work in conjunction with one another and reveals, once again, feng shui's basis in the cycles and elements of the natural world. Eight of the nine parts of bagua are associated with one of the four cardinal directions or the midpoint between them; an area of or issue in human life; and a color. (See drawing.) The cardinal directions are each associated with one of the four elements and a season; the fifth element, earth, is connected

to the bagua's center, the Tai Chi, pictured as a yin-yang. South is associated with summer, recognition and fame, the color red, and the element of fire; north with winter, career and life's journey, the colors blue and black, and the element of water; east with spring, family and health, the color green, and the element of wood; west with autumn, children, the color white, and the element of metal. The area of marriage and relationship is located in the southwest, and associated with the color yellow and sometimes pink; the area of mentors, elders, and benefactors in the northwest and associated with gold, silver, and white; the area of knowledge and education in the northeast, with blue; the southeast with wealth and prosperity and with the color purple.

The relationship of the elements is also central to maintaining good feng shui both inside the home and outside in the garden, because there are both creative (beneficial) and destructive cycles of the elements. In the creative cycle, wood, symbol of growth and creativity, produces fire; fire, signifying heat and energy, creates ash or earth; earth, representing stability, produces metal; metal, representing accumulation, produces water; water, in turn, nourishes wood which begins the cycle anew. In the destructive cycle, though, the elements interact in negative ways: Wood penetrates earth; earth absorbs water; water puts out fire; fire melts metal; metal cuts into wood.

According to Jami Lin, it is important to have representations, some literal and others symbolic, of the five elements—Wood, Earth, Fire, Water, and Metal—present

South
Fire-Red-Summer

Southeast

Southwest

East
Wood-Green-Spring

West
Metal-White-Autumn

Northeast

Northwest

North
Water-Black-Winter

in nature in the appropriate areas of the garden. Wood, the symbol of growth and opportunity, is represented by trees and woody plants. Earth, emblem of stability, is found in paved pathways and stone benches as well as in the boulders and rocks removed from the soil as beds are created. The element of water, associated with clarity as well as wealth, can be represented literally by a water feature, although Jami reminds us that it is very important that the water be clear and that it flows towards you. (Muddied water signifies confusion, while the outward flow tokens the loss of wealth.) In the garden, as Jami points out, fire is sun energy, and the interplay of strong light and shade in the garden can represent fire as can trees in pyramid shapes or shrubs with pyramidal leaves. Finally, the element of metal may be represented by metal objects or, if the garden is thriving, by the plants fed by the minerals in the soil.

Above: *In this garden of spirit, a statue of Confucius graces an area of mentors, but any object or statue that symbolizes inspiration would work equally well.*

Left: *The area of South is strengthened by red plantings, as in this garden designed by Pamela Wood.*

Opposite: *The bagua is oriented with the south at the top (as opposed to the north, as it is in the West) because in China south is the most auspiciuos direction from which prosperity flows. At the very center is the Tai Chi, symbolic of unity and resolution; its element is earth. Remember as you work with the bagua that you are striving for overall balance in the garden; the areas of the bagua are related, as are all the parts of life they represent.*

Working with the specific areas of the garden related to life issues is important to your spiritual well-being, as well as your general prosperity, and you can design your garden using the principles of feng shui. Using color in your planting, for example, to strengthen those areas of life that need attention is one way of restoring spiritual and emotional balance; plant pink and yellow flowers in the area of marriage and relationship (southwest), for example, or make sure that brighter colors don't overwhelm the greens necessary for health and balance in the area of family (east). A row of spectacular sunflowers, emblematic of the element of fire, can enhance the area of fame and recognition (south). Jami suggests using a square divided into nine equal parts, rather than the eight-sided bagua, since it's likely that your garden will be closer to a quadrilateral in shape. Feel free to be creative as you strengthen the various areas of the garden, remembering to keep the center—the Tai Chi representing earth—open so that the chi flows to all parts of the garden. In Jami's own garden she has planted tall trees and red flowers in the south, the area of fame and recognition; since this is the area associated with the element of fire, it is also a fine place for an outdoor grill. The southwest portion,

associated with marriage and relationship, should include pairings of plants or objects; Jami suggests a ficus tree with intertwined trunks or a bench for two. The west, associated with children, is the perfect place to put a child's swing set or sandbox; if you don't have children, you might consider incorporating something playful that brings out the child in you. In the northwest part of the

garden, the area of benefactors, Jami suggests a bird feeder and birdbath to welcome avian spirits. Site a fish pond or water feature in the north, the area of career and journey associated with water; on the other hand, the northeast, the area of knowledge and inspiration, is the ideal place for a garden devoted to meditation. Put a bench here or a statue of a guardian angel or other deity who informs your spirit. The east is the area of family and health and the most propitious site for a table for outdoor gathering. You might also want to plant herbs in the eastern section, choosing plants associated with either culinary use (for the nurturance of family) or healing. In the southeast corner of her Florida garden, the area associated with wealth and fruitfulness, Jami has planted fruit trees; this area can also be strengthened by the addition of a vegetable patch.

Good maintenance in the feng shui garden is absolutely essential to its harmony, and the flow of chi. Landscape designer Mark Leuchten points out that, just as for good feng shui, the front door of the home should not be obstructed to permit the chi to flow in, so, too, access to the garden also needs to be clear. Remove any tree limbs or overgrown shrubs that form an obstruction to the flow of energy; repair cracked paved surfaces. Peeling paint and rotting wood are all impediments to chi and good feng shui. Before designing

Living creatures, such as this turtle (opposite) increase the life energy of the feng shui garden, while both windchimes (above right) and mirrors (opposite far left) help the chi flow freely. The gazing ball can also provide a focal point, giving the viewer yet another perspective on the garden of spirit.

a garden, Mark walks around the house and property, looking for physical and symbolic obstacles; there is, he points out, an important boundary between "ongoing work" and "old debris." It is vital that dead plant material be removed promptly, as well as all manner of clutter—both natural and man-made. Jami Lin tells how, after being on the road for weeks on end, lecturing and teach-

ing, she and her husband began to feel a loss of intimacy and partnership. In her own garden the marriage area is partly occupied by a long-neglected tool shed. It had, as she puts it, "stuff" piled around in and inside of it; she and her husband took the toolshed on as a mutual project, restoring its—and their—balance and harmony. She laughingly points out that even a

feng shui expert sometimes forgets to pay prompt attention to the neglected areas of the garden, with important consequences.

You can also improve the flow of energy in the garden by focusing on the relationship of shapes in the landscape. Linear shapes are yang in nature, while circular ones are yin, and it is best to try to keep them in balance. Using sound can also improve the garden's energy level, either by hanging wind chimes or planting grasses and reeds that rustle in the wind. In addition to plant life, fish in a pond or plants and feeders that encourage wildlife to become a part of your feng shui sanctuary will increase the chi in the garden. Design the areas of the garden with focal points, both to direct the flow of chi and your own attention: Statues and sculptures, a fountain, even a bank of fragrant flowers. Lights anywhere in the garden can also enhance energy, since they represent both fire and the yang nature of the sun (the moon is yin and feminine).

The feng shui garden is a sanctuary that lets us connect to the energy of the cosmos and the larger patterns and cycles that animate it. At the dawn of a new millennium, this art has much to teach us about nature and ourselves, and the enrichment of the spirit.

137

THE *Celtic* GARDEN

I see my life go drifting like a river

From change to change; I have been many things —

A green drop in the surge, a gleam of light

Upon a sword, a fir-tree on a hill...

William Butler Yeats

The Celtic vision of the natural world as sacred space has a unique spirit that still survives in much of European folklore; its legacy is the fairy and the fairy ring, the water sprite and the holy well, the tales of giants and Irish warrior kings such as Cuchulain and Fionn MacCumal. The Celtic garden is one that encourages us to see all things as animate with spirit, whether they are living or not. If we were to assign the Celtic spirit a color, it would be the green of moss, emerging from the shadows of the forest floor; its primary light would be that of the moon—pale, misty, and half-hidden in shadow—even though the Celts also celebrated their sun god, Lug, and his sacred marriage at harvest festivals each year on August 1, and the restorative power of the bonfire was central to their celebrations.

The Celtic spirit is also full of mystery and danger, of spells and divination. In folktales, the druids, both priests and magicians, could not only cause illness or death with their incantatory rites, but create storms and bewildering mists as well. They stopped armies with a "druid's hedge," an invisible but uncrossable barrier that only one of their kind could change. For the Celts the physical and spiritual worlds were one, and this world was closely connected to the world of death; Celtic myths are full of shape-shifters and powerful shamans taught by animal guides. Their beliefs embraced eternal life and an immortal soul, as noted and remarked upon by the Roman Julius Caesar. The holy vessel of pagan Celtic religion was the cauldron, an emblem of spirit that took numerous forms. The first symbolized the divine plenty of earth as well as all knowledge; the Celtic goddess of poetry and the arts, Cerridwen, too had a cauldron, which signified inspiration. The second cauldron was that of rebirth, while the third was that of sacrifice. The liquid contained in the cauldron—often water—too had special magical power. The Celtic reverence for the tree spirits and animals of the forest is preserved for us not only in the rich floral and zoomorphic ornamentation of their household and ritual objects, weapons, and jewelry but in poetry and prose from the Christian era. The Celtic cathedral was the stand of trees, the hill, the river, or the lake; the woodland was home to a pantheon of male and female spirit deities whose roots reached deep into earth and whose branches arched up into the sky. For the Celts, wood signified learning and knowledge (the Celtic words for "wood" and "learning" have the same root). The secret wisdom of the druids was written on the bark of sacred trees, or *ogham*, and among the holiest of trees were the birch, the rowan, the ash, the oak,

Previous pages: *In Stephen Huyler's meditation garden in Maine, the Celtic Green Man, an ancient image of the male aspect of fecundity and consort to the Goddess, literally bursts with the green energy of the vine.*

Above left: *The black birch (Betula lenta) was probably a funerary symbol, perhaps a guardian in life and death.*

Above: *The spirit of autumn is that of changing light as the year veers from harvest to the quiescence of winter.*

the hazel, and the apple. The Celtic vision of nature and the world—saturated with symbol and spirit—survived the eventual triumph of Christianity, resulting in a unique

Above: *The holly and its berries were part of the ancient Irish tree alphabet and were later absorbed into Christian symbolism where they were associated with John the Baptist and Christ and His Passion.*

Above right: *The vision of trees is never static, always changing; here, waterdrops transform the leaves of liriodendron.*

Above far right: *It seems likely that, for the Celts, fire was a symbol of divine energy as well as part of ritual; the feast of Betaine (or "Bel Fires") was celebrated on May 1, the beginning of summer, to bring fruitfulness to the earth and all those who lived on it. To purify the herds, druids built and stoked huge bonfires, through which livestock were driven.*

hybrid of pagan and Christian traditions, of which the Celtic cross is the preeminent example. The circle of the cross is the wheel of the sun god, who crossed the sky in a horse-drawn chariot which, here, is connected to the cruciform, symbol of the Christian Son of God. The standing cross itself probably evolved from the pagan tradition of standing stones or megaliths, which marked sacred sites or were aniconic representations of deities. In many places that were once home to the Celts, particularly in Brittany, megaliths were "converted" to Christian landmarks of faith either through incised carving or by surmounting them with crosses.

Trees inform the spirit of the Celtic garden. The birch tree is the first letter of the ancient Irish Tree Alphabet, and began the Celtic calen-

dar, probably because it was the first tree to leaf out in the forest. According to Robert Graves, birch rods were used ceremonially by the druids to drive out the spirit of the old year; in later centuries birch brooms were considered powerful tools against evil spirits. The whiteness of the tree's bark symbolized its purity. In addition, the birch was probably associated with funerary rites, perhaps because the dead were covered in birch boughs; it may have been, too, that the birch was a guardian spirit that helped prepare the soul for its new life. (Its use in folk medicine too may have been part of its importance.) The rowan and its red berry were also considered sacred; Robert Graves, in *The White Goddess*, tells how in ancient Ireland, before an impending battle, over bonfires of rowan branches, the druids summoned the guardian spirits with incantations. It seems possible that thickets of rowan trees, closely associated with divination, were considered oracular places. The ash was associated with rebirth, as well as with the power of the ocean's waters; its wood yielded the spears for the warrior and the oars of seafarers.

Of all the trees, though, the oak was most holy, as it was in many other cultures, an emblem of endurance, strength, and protection. (In Latin there is a single word signifying both strength and the oak, *robur*.) For the Celts as well as other peoples, the oak was the *axis mundi*, or world tree, thought to be resistant to supernatural forces. The amazing versatility of the oak's wood—it is a superb and strong material for building as well as burning for warmth—in addition to the edibility of its acorn (which was eaten cooked and mashed) made it a natural repository of symbolic value. The druids ate acorns before prophesying; the acorn itself symbolizes the power of the spirit. For the Celts the oak was a symbol of male potency as well as wisdom; according to writer Peter Berresford Ellis, in his book *The Druids*, 150 surviving stone monuments honoring the Celtic "Father of the Gods" are depicted with trees, oak leaves, and acorns. The mistletoe that grew high up on the sacred oak was fecundity incarnate and, since it flourished between earth and heaven without roots, a powerful source of magic. Sacred to the druids as an offering to the gods, mistletoe was harvested by the light of the sixth-day moon with a silver scythe; the ritual sacrifice of two white bulls completed the offering.

The hazel tree, as well as its nut, were of symbolic importance, strongly associated with spiritual and practical wisdom as several interrelated Irish legends make clear. The ties between the tree and holy waters are also strong, and it is no accident that divining and dowsing rods are traditionally made of hazel branches. Legend has it that nine hazel trees, symbolizing all the arts and sciences, overhung Connla's well and, as the nuts fell into the waters,

the salmon swimming there would eat them. The great hero Fionn MacCumal was instructed by his druid teacher to catch and cook a salmon from the river Boyne, a sacred river, but was forbidden to eat it. As he turned the fish he burned his thumb, put it in his mouth, and received the gift of deepest wisdom. Another of the Irish mythical kings was named MacGuill, or "son of the hazel tree."

Two other trees, the elder and the willow, were traditionally associated with witches and witchcraft. The water-loving willow belonged, it was thought, to the moon goddess, and was a tree of enchantment. (Graves notes that the words "witch," "willow," and "wicked" all have the same roots. The baskets that held the victims of druidic sacrifices were made of willow.) The hawthorn was another sacred plant of great power; cutting one down, it was thought, betokened the direst of luck. In Celtic folklore, the fruit or berry has a rich symbolism all of its own, particularly that of the apple tree, called the "noblest tree of all" in ancient Celtic poetry. The apple symbolized immortality; Avalon, where the hero King Arthur was magically healed, means "the island of apple trees."

The Celtic garden takes its spirit from the natural woodland, giving us an opportunity to get in touch with the magical and mystical aspects of the cycle of nature; in this sacred space, the art of cultivation is subtle, permitting us to see the wildness of nature. Its sense of sanctuary is based in the canopy that the branches of trees provide, in the filtered light and light raindrops that nourish the plants growing at the base of trees. The web of life is evident in a variety of ways in this garden, as we begin to appreciate the shelter and protection trees provide to other flora. The Celtic garden is one that teaches the value and beauty of shade, and reminds us that the woodland, not the open meadow, is nature's model. What twentieth-century science has confirmed—the centrality of trees to the oxygen-replenished ecosystem in which living beings thrive—the ancient lore of the Celts expressed in spiritual and symbolic terms. Their understanding of the tree as a wise elder who represents collective wisdom is still valuable to us today; the trees we plant and tend will stay on as reminders of our presence on earth long after we are gone. The Celtic vision of the tree, rooted in earth and reaching toward sky, remains the perfect metaphor for the awakened spirituality we can achieve in the garden.

In the Celtic garden we turn to the elements of the natural landscape for inspiration. Celtic knotwork—intricate patterns of sacred geometry—seems to have found inspiration in the vine, curling upon itself and embracing whatever it grows on. The shamrock—the emblem of Ireland and of the Celts—as well as clover and other three-leafed plants were holy to the druids, and became

Opposite: *The power of the sun, captured in a garden mosaic.*

Right: *Fairy rings of mushrooms, long thought to mark where fairies danced, were endowed with a special kind of magic.*

Christian emblems of the Trinity; they, too, can be made a part of the contemporary Celtic garden. A water feature—preferably one in a free-form, natural shape—can echo the sacrality of the well and the spring in Ireland, Scotland, Wales, Brittany, and all the other places the Celtic spirit flourished. Water for the Celts had a magical, supernatural character; wells were known to restore the lives of slain warriors, while in Wales the "fair people," or fairies, inhabited streams and lakes, and were thought to dance under the light of the full moon. Irish folktales reveal that the druids could change the course of waters—diverting them in punishment or bestowing them in gratitude.

Using statuary in the Celtic garden can reinforce the symbolism inherent in the natural landscape. Crosses, knotwork, and statues and containers in the shapes of animals—a swan planter, for example—reinforce the Celtic notion of spirit in all things. Many different animals were sacred to the Celts, among them birds, dogs, deer, and horses.

The Celtic sanctuary encourages us to experience the magic and the mystery of nature; it is a place where, as night falls, the shadow of a fairy's wings might well be glimpsed.

THE *Biblical* GARDEN

And God said, Let the earth bring forth

grass, the herb yielding seed, and the

fruit tree yielding fruit after his kind,

whose seed was in itself, after his kind:

and God saw that it was good.

Genesis, I:11

The spiritual landscape takes on another form in the Biblical garden, one that links our present-day lives in both literal and symbolic ways to the events and the people described in the Old and New Testaments. The book of Genesis recounts God's creation of the plants on the third day and how, on the sixth day, He established the hegemony of man, to whom "the herb bearing seeds" and "the fruit of a tree yielding seed" shall be "as meat." In the Old and New Testaments, the role of gardens—Eden, Solomon's sanctuary of beauty, Gethsemane, the garden in which Jesus is laid in the sepulchre, or that mentioned in Revelations—and natural landscapes goes far

the tree, and the field were their and their livestock's source of sustenance, and their symbolic power in the Bible was a direct reflection of its real, everyday importance. God's continuing presence was indicated not only by the landscape and its plants—He appeared to Moses from within the burning bush on the holy mountain, Horeb, and the bush miraculously was not consumed—but by all manner of natural phenomena, from the seasons and beneficial rains to the forces of destruction that affected the crops. In Deuteronomy the reward for adherence to God's commandments is expressed in terms of the seasons,

planting, and harvest: "That I will give the rain in his due season, the first rain and the latter rain, that thou mayst gather in thy corn, and thy wine, and thine oil." Equally, turning away from God had consequences no farmer or shepherd could fail to understand: "that there shall be no rain, and the land yield not her fruit." The fecundity of the natural world and the flourishing of the garden that sustained body and soul are, again and again, the measurements of a good and happy life: "Thy wife shall be as a fruitful vine by the sides of thine house; thy children like olive plants round about thy table" (Psalms 128:3)

beyond providing scenery for events. Plants and their husbandry (as well as flocks and shepherding) are often the symbolic context used to convey spiritual ideas and messages, precisely because, to these farmers and herders, the land on which they lived and worked was as familiar as the creases of their palms. The fruits of the vine,

Above: *Wormwood* (Artemisia absinthium) *is mentioned a number of times in the Bible, usually with references to its bitterness; metaphorically, the plant stands for suffering.*

Right: *The Bible Garden at the Cathedral of St. John the Divine.*

Previous pages: *At the Rodef Shalom Biblical Botanical Garden in Pittsburgh, the area respresenting the River Jordan is planted with papyrus and blue flag.*

or "In that day, saith the Lord of hosts, shall ye call every man his neighbor under the vine and under the fig tree" (Zachariah 3:10).

The extraordinary connection forged between spirit and nature is nowhere more evident than in the fascinating insight offered into the origins of the menorah, the 3,000-year-old symbol of the Jewish faith and people and the emblem of Israel. The description of the seven-branched menorah (its name simply means "candalabrum" in Hebrew) and its gift to Moses by God on Mt. Sinai are detailed in Exodus 25:31–40. The text is, as Nogah Hareuveini, author of *The Ecology of the Bible*, writes,"striking in its use of botanical details," and the natural models for the menorah have been identified as members of the sage or salvia family, which grows all over the Holy Land; it is thought, too, that the most fragrant types, such as *Salvia dominica* and *Salvia palaestina*, were probably also burned as incense at the altar. The menorah and the altar incense are always mentioned in combination.

In the New Testament, too, the vocabulary both of nature and of cultivation—planting, tending, and harvesting—is used by Jesus to explain the spirit of the new dispensation. Jesus himself is "the true vine, and my Father is the husband-

men," while God's children are "the branches." The parable of the mustard seed explains the Kingdom of God as a reflection of the small miracle of planting and germination: "It is like a grain of mustard seed, which a man took, and cast into his garden; and it grew, and waxed a great tree; and the fowls of the air lodged in the branches of it." The

Above: *Because of their fruits, the date palm and the pomegranate, among other trees, symbolized the blessings bestowed on humanity by God. The calyx of the pomegranate's fruit served as the model for the ornament carved on King Solomon's Temple and those embroidered on Aaron's priestly robes. The date palm grew in desert oases, and thus signalled the presence of water. In Exodus, the oases of Elim means "sacred trees."*

birds, here, are emblems of the spirit. Images, too, of fruit-bearing trees explain the nature of goodness, the inseparability of the inner spirit and the outer self: "For a good tree bringeth not forth corrupt fruit; neither doth a corrupt tree bring forth good fruit. For every tree is known by his own fruit. For of thorns, men do not gather figs, nor of a bramble bush gather they grapes." Even the nature of faith is explained by Jesus in terms of husbandry.

Historically, the many different plants mentioned in both the Old and New Testaments, as well as the specific imagery of the Song of Solomon, inspired the gardens of the Middle Ages, within both monastery and castle walls: "A garden enclosed is my sister, my spouse; a spring shut up; a fountain sealed. . . A fountain of gardens, a well of living waters, and streams from Lebanon." These "gardens enclosed" were understood as images of Paradise, places of rest and seclusion, deliberately set off from the corruption of the mundane world. Planted with both medicinal and culinary plants—many drawn from the pages of Scripture or from legends pertaining to the events in the life of Jesus or the Virgin Mary, or other saints—they also incorporated symbolic elements of design.

A contemporary, enclosed Bible garden at Christ Church in Port

Republic, Maryland, provides, according to Nancy Thompson, a parishioner and horiculturist who cares for it, a "quiet place for meditation" next to the church's parish hall. This biblical garden was designed 30 years ago and consists of two rooms, the first of which is a walled garden, some 20 by 30 feet. On one of its walls is a fountain—a design of three shells that spill out into a small, semicircular pool, filled with water lilies, papyrus, and fish. Next to the fountain is a plaque inscribed with words from Psalms 46:10: "Be still and know that I am God." The pathways are laid in the shape of a cross; in the center stands a beautiful Celtic cross, carved out of red oak. There are two

Above: *Symbol of power and strength, the cedar of Lebanon was the wood used to build King Solomon's Temple.*

benches for meditation; plants drawn from the Bible—among them a grape vine, a fig tree, and liriope lilies—grow alongside small boxwood. A passageway leads to the "outer" room of the garden, this one 40 by 30 feet. Nancy points out that there is still some disagreement among scholars about the exact identification of certain plants in the Bible; for example, it's well-known that the "lilies of the field" are not lilies at all (they are narcissus) and that the rose of Sharon is, in fact, a tulip native to the Holy Land. In selecting plants, too, Nancy has to compensate for the Maryland climate. Among those planted here are wormwood, mint, sage, rosemary, marjoram, love-in-a-mist, hyssop, leek, coriander, chamomile, a weeping mulberry (the "sycamore" of the

Bible), cucumber, pomegranate, rue, star of Bethlehem, apricot, cedar of Lebanon, juniper, and storax (once used as incense). In all, 50 different plants, identified both by their scientific names and by the biblical reference, are displayed here.

And while it is true that some of the plants included in the Bible garden are "exotic," serving to bring the experience of the Holy Land home to American soil, many of them are, in fact, relatively common. Paul Heimbach, the curator of the Warsaw Biblical Garden in Indiana,

Above and opposite: *At the Rodef Shalom Biblical Botanical Garden, blue flag (**Iris versicolor**), water lilies and lotuses, and yellow flag (**Iris pseudocaorus**). Yellow flag is probably one of the flowers referred to, in the Bible, as "lilies of the river."*

comments that the beauty of certain plants is underscored by "their association with the inspiring and educational stories of the Bible"; a Bible garden, he notes, permits people to develop a new "relationship" with "ordinary" plants endowed with important meaning in Scripture. Among the common plants and trees that acquire new meaning in the context of a Bible garden are herbs such as garlic, dill, coriander, and sage; trees such as pine and willow; and flowers such as nigella, sternbergia, mallow, and loosestrife.

The symbolism in a Bible garden extends beyond its plantings. At the Rodef Sholem Biblical Garden in Pittburgh, for example, the site is actually shaped like the land of Israel, with features symbolic of its actual topography: A waterfall sug-

gests the source of the river Jordan high in the mountains, while a stream that runs through the entire garden is the Jordan itself; a large pond, filled with papyrus and lotus, stands for the Sea of Galilee; and bubbling springs suggest En Gedi at the Dead Sea. Throughout this garden, specific plantings allude to Old Testament details and events. Among them are the date palm (*Phoenix dactylifera*), symbol of peace and prosperity, which may well be the tree of life in the Bible; myrtle (*Myrtus communis*), one of the plants used in the Jewish festival of Sukkoth, and symbolic of divine generosity; sorghum (*Sorghum bicolor*) which may be the "parched corn" Boaz gave to Ruth; and dandelion (*Taraxacum officinale*), one of the bitter herbs of the Passover Seder.

Planting a biblical garden brings a new dimension to the words of the Scriptures, and allows us to incorporate the message of the Bible into our everyday lives in a concrete way. Even a corner of a garden planted with herbs and flowers drawn from the Bible can become a special place of contemplation and rest, one that honors God's presence in our homes and gardens. As James Martineau, a renowned nineteenth-century minister, once preached, "Nothing less than the majesty of God, and the powers of the world to come, can maintain the peace and sanctity of our homes, the order and serenity of our minds, the spirit of patience and tender mercy in our hearts." It must have been an oversight that he didn't mention the peace of the garden.

THE *Saint's* GARDEN

Earth's crammed with Heaven,

And every common bush afire with God.

Elizabeth Barrett Browning

 The Saint's garden is a different kind of oasis, a place of peace devoted to beauty where a vision of God reveals itself in the details of nature, and where the saint's spirit and philosphy imbue the garden with a specific character. Meant as a sanctuary where we can come into contact with the divine through prayer, meditation, and the example of the saint as spiritual mentor, this garden is based in 2,000 years of traditional Christian story and symbolism. Statuary plays an important role in this garden as do other objects that reflect the nature of the saint's life and spiritual teachings; this is a space that is devoted equally to contemplation of God and meaningful activity. Tending to the garden—watering, weeding, maintaining—is, in this context, an act that brings us closer to God and the meaning of His creation.

Preeminent among the saints associated with the garden and nature is the Virgin Mary, mother of Jesus, the embodiment of nurturance and maternality. By creating a garden dedicated to her, we acknowledge gardening as an act of nurturance and honor the qualities Mary embodies: comfort, compassion, understanding. Just as she shelters humanity as the Mother of Mercy and Our Lady of Perpetual Help, so, too, in her spiritual

garden we focus on our role as stewards of our plots. The Virgin Mary is also the guardian of growth, both spiritual and material: May is Mary's month precisely because of its burgeoning fecundity—what Gerard Manley Hopkins called "this ecstasy all through mothering earth." In this garden, the Virgin Mary's traditional symbols are reminders of the cosmic order: she is associated with the returning moon as an emblem of her continuing sustenance and the light that breaks up the darkness of night and spiritual ignorance; she is clothed with the rays of the sun because her Son is the source of all true illumination. In this sacred space, enclosures, gates, and fountains take on profound symbolic meaning. The enclosed garden, an

Above: *A meditation bench, nestled under the branches of an oak tree, is flanked by a statue of the Virgin Mary, opening the vistas ahead in more ways than one at Mount Calvary in Santa Barbara, California.*

Previous pages: *Surrounded by pansies and roses, a beautiful statue of the Virgin Mary transforms the landcape at the Mount Manresea Jesuit Retreat House in Staten Island, New York.*

image drawn from the Song of Solomon, has stood for Mary herself, a reference to her Immaculate Conception as well as the mystery of the Annunciation; she is equally the Fountain of Life invoked by the words of the thirty-sixth Psalm, "For with thee is the fountain of light; in thy light shall we see light." As the Virgin Mother, she is the closed gate mentioned in Ezekiel. Including any of these elements in the garden's design increases its meaningfulness.

The extraordinary number of flowers and plants associated with the Virgin Mary—most drawn from legends and stories connected to events in her life—teach us that if Mary herself is a garden enclosed, then much that is wild or cultivated, growing within and outside of the garden walls, reflects her spirit as well. This garden can encompass a wide range of plants chosen for beauty, symbolic meaning, and season. Because the blooming of certain flowers marked the celebration of events in the Marian year, they were used as objects of meditation and remembrance by friars and monks as a natural calendar: the white snowdrop (*Galanthus* sp.) was the flower of Candlemas; the Madonna lily (*Lilium candidium*) and Our Lady's smock (*Cardamine pratensis*) tokened the Annunciation; the Greek anemone (*Anemone blanda*) recalled the Passion; Virgin's bower (*Clematis virginiana*) was the flower of the Assumption.

But no sanctuary devoted to the Virgin Mary would be complete without the presence of a single rosebush, a bower of roses, or a cascade of climbing roses grown along a fence or wall. In the words of Cardinal Henry Newman, Mary is "the queen of spiritual flowers, and therefore she is called the rose, for the rose is fitly called of all the flowers the most beautiful. But moreover, she is the mystical or hidden rose, for mystical means hidden." Mary is also the thornless rose, born without original sin. The sweet fragrance of the rose, along with the scents of other flowers such as jasmine, was an emblem of the beauty of her spirit.

Mary's garden is a place of quiet, where the central mystery of Christian faith, Christ's Resurrection, can be celebrated in terms of the feminine. Set off from the mundane world, Mary's garden is also a place of retreat.

Designing a sanctuary devoted to St. Francis of Assisi is to plan a garden celebrating the variety of God's creation and the vitality of all things living. This spiritual garden is a joyous enclave, a shout of praise to heaven, full of color and scent, butterflies and birds, sound and motion. St. Francis, the twelfth-century founder of the monastic order that bears his name, was born wealthy, yet in his early twenties he turned his back on worldly things and embraced a life of absolute poverty. His life was marked by devotion to all of humanity, full of fervor and religious commitment; his love of nature was so great that he once preached to the sparrows at Alviano and saved the town of Gubbio from the ravages of a wolf simply by speaking to the wolf and calling him "Brother." The humble lark was St. Francis's favorite, and it was said that when the saint died, a great exaltation of larks circled the house in which he lay, an avian image of eternity in motion, and sang his praises.

This garden is a place of sanctuary for wildlife, a refuge where God is fully visible in the details; while it is a cultivated space, it teaches us, first and foremost, to pull back from altering the patterns of nature as much as we can. The hallmarks of the suburban landscape—broad expanses of lawn, clipped evergreens, and flowers free of pollen and fruit—are not a part of this sanctuary. While you can choose plants for beauty and color (butterflies don't care about color, as it happens), for this garden, other considerations take precedence. You will want to choose your roses not for elegance but for the production of hips for the

birds; try *Rosa rugosa*, *Rosa canina*, or *Rosa carolina*. If you are planting to attract birds, thinking seasonally will assure a steady stream of these symbols of soul and spirit: plant barberry (*Berberis* sp.) and winterberry (*Ilex vertcillata*) for their berries in late winter, winter honeysuckle (*Lonicera fragrantissima*) for its bright-red fruit in early spring, and viburnum (*Viburnum* sp.) for an avian delight in late summer and early fall. Feed your soul and the seed-eaters by planting sunflower, coreopsis, cosmos, and millet. Red tubular flowers such as trumpet creeper will please the hummingbirds, although they'll also feast from honeysuckle, sweet William, and other flowers.

Right: *St. Francis's special connection to all of God's creation is reflected in this statue in a Midwest garden, representing his taming of the wolf of Gubbio.*

Each aspect of this garden's design and its plantings contributes to its sense of harmony, so that the human visitor can throw open the windows of the soul. In addition to a statue of St. Francis, this sanctuary should include a bench or seating far enough from the plantings so as not to disturb its winged visitors, a source of water (a bird or butterfly bath), ample natural shelter in the form of shrubs and vines, as well as "wild" or deliberately uncultivated areas. (To attract butterflies to the garden, you will also need to supply the butterfly larvae with a source of food appropriate to the species that live in your region, and some butterfly larvae are very picky. Those of the monarch butterfly, for example, feed only on members of the milkweed family, Asclepius. For more information, please see page 177.)

Since St. Francis was a steward of both the earth and the human soul, the lesson of this space dedicated to him is to let go of our worldly concerns and begin to see both the natural and human communities as one. Surrounded by beauty and quiet, we use the time spent here to connect to others in spirit, both those close to us and less fortunate strangers. It is a place where, following the example of St. Francis, we learn charity in the true sense.

St. Fiacre's garden, celebrates healing, reflected in the therapeutic activity of growing and tending, the quieting effect of nature, and the medicinal qualities of the plants

Above: *Crowned, as befits the Queen of Heaven, her Son in her arms, this beautifully rendered statue of the Virgin makes this New York garden a special kind of sanctuary.*

grown in it. Because Fiacre is also known as the "saint of the spade," in this garden the everyday implement symbolizes the spiritual component of gardening. Fiacre, an Irish prince who lived in the sixth century, joined a monastery near Paris, France, but, after several years of communal living decided that the life of the hermit would permit him to communicate with God more fully. He retired to the woods where he built a simple hut and fashioned a garden that would provide him with sustenance. Over time his reputation as a healer of both body and soul grew, and more and more people sought him out for spiritual and physical help. Many miracles were attributed to him and, after his death in 670 A.D., the Benedictine priory where he was buried became a place of pilgrimage for the sick and infirm. Plant this sacred space with herbs having both a spiritual and medicinal history, such as hyssop, sage, passionflower, camomile, lavender, and echinacea (for more suggestions, see page 88, "The Healing Garden"). Doing the work of gardening is part of the healing process in this sacred space, as is quiet contemplation.

Many other saints can inspire the spirit of the garden; you may wish to choose to honor a saint who embodies a spiritual quality you admire, or one who is a patron of an activity that has special meaning for you. (For researching specific saints, see Resources, page 180.) For example, to celebrate the music of nature, dedicate your sacred space to the patron saint of music, St. Cecilia, and add plants as well as feeders to attract avian friends; you can also plant grasses which create a natural "music" of their own, or hang windchimes from branches and trellises. Traditional

Christian symbols and objects such as the Greek and Latin crosses. bells, candles, water basins, and other religious artifacts can also be used to great effect in any of these gardens. (For more, see "Gardening for the Soul," page 8, "The Biblical Garden," page 144, and "The Celtic Garden, page 138.) Remember, as you work, the words of Romans 8:6: "To be spiritually minded is life and peace."

Just as the enclosed garden is a symbol of Mary herself, so, too, many flowers are associated with her, from the grandeur of the rose to the humble violet. Here, a sampling: Our Lady's nightcap of Canterbury bells (Campanula medium, above); the rose (top right); Our Lady's mantle (Alchemilla mollis, center right); and Our Lady's slipper (Cypripedium sp., bottom right).

THE *Labyrinth* GARDEN

…no journey carries one far unless,

as it extends into the world around us, it gives us

equal distance into the world within.

Lillian Smith

In the labyrinth garden sacred space takes on a specific geometric form, and the landscape is deliberately shaped and changed to create a tool for spiritual awakening and transformation. In these gardens, walking the labyrinth is the primary spiritual exercise. Precisely because walking is a kinesthetic experience—engaging our senses, muscles, and nerves—walking the labyrinth brings body and spirit together in a literal and concrete way, breaking down the distinction between activity and contemplation, and encouraging us to consider everyday activity—even a simple walk—as spiritual in nature. Because there are so many different ways the pattern of the labyrinth can be articulated—by paved walkways of stone or brick, through the use of raised beds or simple paths marked by rocks, by mowing the design onto a grassy field or by mounding a "sculpted" pathway, or even by creating a temporary labyrinth with the spray paint used for football

fields—the labyrinth garden can be adapted for use in almost any outdoor space, large or small. Even its design is flexible, and can be varied to satisfy both the requirements of the physical space and individual needs.

Creating a labyrinth garden connects us to thousands of years of spiritual history. This ancient form, which is at least five millennia old, is probably closely related both to the naturally labyrinthine caves of the early Paleolithic which served as humanity's first places of worship and the vocabulary of sacred symbols incised on cave walls, pottery, and statuary—labyrinthine patterns, spirals, and meanders among them—which were used to denote the life force or the divine. Unlike a maze which functions as a three-dimensional puzzle—a construction that alternates "true" paths and dead ends, and where the builder's goal is to disorient the person trying to find his way out, either through high walls or shubbery—the labyrinth is composed of a series of courses leading to a central point. There are no "wrong" turns or impediments to the path;

as labyrinth designer Alex Champion notes, "It is a straight line that has been worked on." The symbolism of the labyrinth's shape—a journey into the center and then out again—suggests that in ancient cultures it was used for a variety of ritual purposes such as the reenactment of birth, the celebration of seasonal rites, or the journey from this world into the underworld. (The labyrinths of megalithic tombs in Egypt, for example, were probably meant both to keep the uninitiated away from the deified king's tomb and to designate the sacred space of the tomb itself.) The center of the labyrinth could signify a place of mystery, of rebirth, of revelation, or self-knowledge. The appearance of the labyrinth in so many different sacred traditions, including the kabbalistic Tree of Life and the Native American "Man in the Maze," underscores both its symbolic and spiritual importance. While the labyrinth, whether rendered in two or three dimensions, is meant to be entered rather than simply contemplated, it is also related to other sacred forms based in geometry, such as the mandalas of Tibetan Buddhism and the sand paintings of the Navajos.

The word "labyrinth," first used by the Greek historian Herodotus in the fifth century B.C., probably comes from *labrys*, or "double ax," the ritual tool of Minoan civilization. Labyrinth means "house of the double ax," and it seems likely that the original labyrinth at Knossos was, according to Vincent Scully in his masterful book *The Earth, the Temple, and the Gods*, a place of ritual dedicated to honoring ancient goddesses closely connected to the earth and nature. The seven-circuit labyrinth now known as "Cretan"—the design of which survives on coins and other artifacts from Minoan civilization circa 1500 B.C.—may have been literally realized by this culture and connected to rites now lost to us.

Labyrinths also have a Christian history. During the Middle Ages, labyrinthine designs—inscribed onto the floors of cathedrals such as Chartres—were used as symbolic places of pilgrimage as well as of penance; churchgoers would travel the labyrinth on their knees, a humble reenactment of a pilgrimage to the Holy Land. (Once again, this use of the labyrinth deliberately blurred the boundaries between body and soul, activity and contemplation. Penance and pilgrimage were physically experienced; at Chartres, even though the labyrinth itself is only 42 feet across, the journey through the labyrinth was over 850 feet in length. To envision how the "pilgrims" on the path felt, we need simply imagine crawling the length of almost three football fields on our knees.)

The recovery of the labyrinth's potential as a spiritual tool over the last decade, due in no small part to the groundbreaking work of Dr. Lauren Artress at Grace Cathedral in San Francisco, has inspired both religious communities and home gardeners to incorporate the labyrinth into indoor and outdoor space. Helen Curry, a labyrinth designer, president of the Labyrinth Society, and founder of the Labyrinth Project of Connecticut,

Previous pages: *The labyrinth at Satsong, with its ladder sculpture, symbolically connecting the earth's center, or omphalos, to the sky.*

Opposite: *Alex Champion's labyrinth in early spring, abloom with daffodils.*

Above: *The form of the labrys itself is part of the design in this labyrinth, based on but larger than that at Chartres, at a retreat center in California, where it is used for meditation. The labyrinth is 56 feet across, with two-foot-wide paths made of decomposed granite.*

acknowledges that while "each of us experiences walking the labyrinth in a unique way, generally, labyrinths refocus our attention on the landscape. The very nature of labyrinth walking gives us an opportunity to take an equal number of right- and left-hand turns. As we walk out of the labyrinth we are literally and symbolically turned around in our environment." Helen points out, too, that there are three stages to the spiritual process of walking the labyrinth: "The time on the way in is preparation; the time at the center is enlightenment or illumination; the time on the way out permits us to reintegrate into the world that which we have received." The Reverend Diana Clark, rector of St. John's Episcopal Church in Montclair, New Jersey, which uses a painted-canvas 11-circuit labyrinth, concurs, adding that "the journey in begins with a stripping away. Next, by trusting the path of the labyrinth, we access the unconscious on the way to the center. At the center of the labyrinth we encounter what Meister Eckhardt called the 'dazzling dark,' or mystery. Coming back out, we are reunited with the world." Reverend Clark notes that, as a spiritual tool, the labyrinth can be used in myriad ways. Some people use it as a pathway for meditation or prayer, sometimes with

The design of the pavement labyrinth at Chartres, laid at the beginning of the 13th century. At its center is a rose shape, representing both the mystical and the Virgin Mary, to whom the cathedral is dedicated. There are 10 labryses in the design.

rosaries or prayer beads; still others simply walk it, enjoying the feeling of being grounded, or use the time in the labyrinth to review their lives. Others enter the labyrinth with a question, and employ the silence and the path to let their inner selves supply the answer.

Marty Cain, an environmental sculptor and labyrinth designer, created her first public labyrinth at Harvard and Radcliffe colleges in 1990. From that first temporary labyrinth—a seven-circuit pattern 60 feet across with three-foot-wide pathways spray-painted onto the quadrangle to honor the earth and open space—she has gone on to design more than 80 labyrinths for public and personal use, both in

cityscapes and in the countryside, on plots large and small. Her own garden, on the side of a New Hampshire farmhouse that once belonged to her grandmother, contains a meander labyrinth, some 40 feet long and 18 feet wide. The 18-inch path is lined by raised beds, three feet wide, in which she grows a potpourri of flowers and vegetables every season, among them lilies, sunflowers, violets and johnny-jump-ups, asters, hollyhocks (which her grandmother started in this garden), Native American tomatoes, cabbage, sweet peas, and runner beans. Lilacs and rosebushes frame this sacred space as well. The entrance to the labyrinth is marked by a birdbath, flanked by a circular bed of herbs; at the other end of the labyrinth is a stone bench Marty uses for meditation. Although Marty travels extensively, when she is home she walks the garden path, sometimes meditating and other times "walking and weeding," a different kind of spiritual exercise.

The essential mystery of the labyrinth and the important, if anecdotal, evidence of its ability to heal both physically and spiritually continue to inform Marty's commitment. Before installing a labyrinth, she dowses and asks the earth if a labyrinth is appropriate to the space. Some of her experiences cannot be explained by reason alone; she recalls installing a seven-circuit labyrinth in the woods north of Athens, Georgia. Surrounded by trees, the labyrinth had a large pillar-shaped loblolly pine tree at its center, growing on a hump of land between two small streams. Once the pathways of the labyrinth had been marked with stones, Marty and her coworkers walked the circuit to bless it, singing a Tibetan chant. Even though there was no wind or breeze, the tree swayed as they chanted; when they stopped, Marty reports, "the tree came to stillness."

In Cambridge, Massacusetts, a labyrinth, which Marty designed and owner Christy Dennis executed, graces a garden setting dominated by trees in a fenced-in quarter-acre yard. The seven-circuit Cretan design, some 24 feet in diameter, is marked by a circular brick path edged with white-flowering vinca. Last year Christy scattered forget-me-not seeds among the bricks and months later the labyrinth was cov-

ered in a blaze of blue, nearly hiding its brick pathways from sight. Christy's love of trees is evident everywhere: A glorious copper beech, which sheds its leaves early in December, stands at the entrance to the garden, and the labyrinth itself, in the eastern corner of the yard, is framed by three apple trees that bend over it and dapple the sunlight. Nearby are fragrant azalea, viburnum, and dogwood trees. Opposite the labyrinth is a short stone path that runs between an herb garden— planted with lavender, basil, thyme, mint, and rhubarb—and a patch of strawberries, blueberries, and raspberries. Two fruit-bearing trees—an Italian plum and a peach—yield luscious harvests. Another path, this one on the east side of the garden, leads to a small terrace and seating area; here Christy has planted a rock garden, along with a Russian olive tree, some young birches with silvery bark, and a pear tree.

Christy remarks that the labryinth has "made the garden more fruitful, almost as though there were beehives or a source of water in it." Walking the labyrinth has made her feel more integrated into the

Left: A private labyrinth echoes the form of the landscape beyond it, making the journey of walking it a metaphor for other journeys.

garden; she has, as she puts it, "an increased appreciation of what's around me, and walking the labyrinth lets me acquaint myself with the details of the garden—the daily changes in buds and bark—in a different way." Even the physical work of laying the bricks for the labyrinth, with the help of a few friends, was transformative, a task that she felt shaped her as she shaped it. Her relationship with the natural

Above: *Focusing on labyrinthine forms in nature—such as the marvelous intricacy of the* **Aloe polyphylia**—*can also help us capture the sense of mystery and revelation we learn from the labyrinth walk (opposite).*

world of the garden has become more interactive; in fact she has started keeping a journal, focused on her pear tree.

On the West Coast Dr. Alex Champion has been building public and private earthwork labyrinths— "sculptures" in the earth using sunken paths and elevated mounds— for over a decade. His own labyrinth in the front yard of his home in California is essentially circular in form, a path with a branch point that can be walked again and again as a "walking meditation." Set in a small area, the entire earthwork is only 16 by 20 feet, but the pathway is 70 feet long. In this labyrinth the 21-inch-wide pathways are lined with stone, and the barriers defining the path are planted with lobelia, pink and white dianthus, red fescue, chamomile, sweet allysum, daffodils, and grasses. Borrowing from an English tradition, Alex left a deliber-ately unplanted wild spot in the garden for nature spirits which, while occupied by relatively undis-tinguished crabgrass, has what he calls a "special glow." This small labyrinth can be walked in each of the cardinal directions, considered sacred in many different cultures, adding to the walk's balancing and soothing effect.

Much more grandiose in scale is the Cretan labyrinth Alex built in

Mendocino County, California. This amazing earthwork—some 60 feet in diameter (the journey into its center and out is just under a quarter mile)—has a pathway depth of a foot to a foot and a half. This depth, Alex notes, gives the feeling, as the labyrinth is walked, "of being in the earth" since the surrounding ground level is higher. Alex continues: "The deeper the pathway, the stronger the feeling. I feel secure when walking it—the round barriers are protective walls from the outside. Time seems to slow down while I'm in the labyrinth and, when I'm at the cen-ter, the outside seems far away. I am in a separate time and space."

In the high desert of New Mexico, surrounded by mountains, a seven-circuit Cretan labyrinth designed by Alex has enhanced the lives of Sonia Hodson and Bill Enoch in many ways. Their labyrinth, 48 feet in diameter with a pathway 450 feet in length, was built to honor the land once peopled by the Apache, the Tewa, and the Anasazi, and its long sacred history. Evidence of this his-tory still surrounds the site: in the petroglyphs still visible on the canyon walls; in the sacred moun-tains and outcroppings of rock once held to be holy (and still looking, in Sonia's words, like "ruined cathe-drals"); and, on the mesas, in the remains of Indian "rock gardens," rectangles defined by a straight line of stones within which seeds were planted to keep in the small amount of moisture nature provided.

Their first exposure to the concept of the labyrinth took place thousands of miles away, in Ireland and Scotland, where the symbol's connection to the sacred became evident to them; further research convinced them of the universal meaning of this sacred form in many cultures, among them that of the Hopi, whose symbol for the Earth Mother was a labyrinth, representing birth and rebirth. As stewards of the land, Sonia and Bill felt that the labyrinth was an appropriate way to "honor the connection between humanity and nature, as well as to honor the caretakers who came before them." Because it is used as a place of ceremony and ritual, they have named their labyrinth Tápu'at, the Hopi word for "Earth Mother." The small town in which they live, Abiquiu, is some 6,400 feet above sea level, has 300 days of sun, and little moisture; even though the sandy soil is inhospitable to cultivation, Sonia and Bill planted fuchsia-colored ice plants to cover the labyrinth, which proved to be an irresistible temptation to rabbits and other creatures. Word of mouth has brought many different people to the full moon and solstice ceremonies they celebrate at

the labyrinth and, as Bill Enoch explains it, these labyrinth walks provide a powerful metaphor for the process that is life: "Even though, within the labyrinth, people appear to be walking in opposite directions, they are, in fact, on their way to the same place."

The way in which the labyrinth can both quiet the soul through the reassurance of a walk without wrong turns and access the inner self has made it a tool of healing as well in different places in the country. Dr. Jennifer Choate, an oncologist in California, has a 10-foot labyrinth planted with chamomile so that the footfalls of her patients release the plants' scents. She finds the labyrinth's symmetry—it is a vesica triangle—grounds, reassures, and calms her patients at a devastating time in their lives. At Satsong, an alternative healing center in Petaluma, California, a 99-foot Cretan labyrinth planted with fescue is situated on a knoll, overlooking a five-acre lake. At the very center of the labyrinth is a sculpture of a twisted ladder, which, Satsong's founder, Kristina Flanaghan, notes, connects the labyrinth's center with the sky. Many different forms of healing have been attributed to the labyrinth; in fact, Kristina feels that the presence of the labyrinth, on what were once the ceremonial

grounds of the native Miwoc peoples, has healed and restored the environment around it. She points to the variety of creatures that have found Satsong to be a haven, among them a blue heron whose mate was cruelly shot by an unknown gunman. Because blue herons mate for life, the male initially left Satsong, only to return a year later; he has been joined by rare black-and-white swans and an eagle who comes to fish in the big pond.

The journey of spirit becomes literally realized by incorporating a labyrinth into your garden. Remember this ancient form can be created in the simplest of ways— using pebbles and stones—and need not even be permanent. (Cornmeal is the perfect, biodegradable medium for a temporary labyrinth.) Creating the labyrinth with others is also a way of sharing the spiritual journey of life.

Gardening as a Spiritual Exercise

It is not graceful and it makes one hot, but it is a

blessed sort of work, and if Eve had had a spade in

Paradise, and known what to do with it, we should

not have had all that sad business of the apple.

Countess von Arnim

PLANNING THE SPIRITUAL GARDEN

Planning and designing the sanctuary garden help to artic-ulate individual spiritual goals. First you need to think about the ways in which you connect to spirit outdoors, whether you decide to act as a garden designer yourself or engage the services of a professional. As you begin to con-sider the garden's design, take into account not only the way you intend to use the space but also the time and effort you are willing to commit to both the execution of the design and the garden's maintenance. The physical tasks of gardening—preparing the soil, seeding, watering, fertiliz-ing, weeding, harvesting—connect us to the life of the garden and are exercises that increase our mindfulness, but it's important that, in making room for the soul outdoors, you assess your commitment realistically and directly.

Ask yourself how much time you're able or willing to devote to tending your garden. If you feel most connected to spirit by actively participating in the cycle of growth, your hands in the dirt, and have the time, then a garden of spirit that is comparatively large and labor intensive will be right for you. Working to sustain the garden will sustain you in different ways. On the other hand, if you already

> ## Those who contemplate the beauty of the earth find reserves of strength that will endure as long as life lasts.
>
> *Rachel Carson*

feel overloaded in your life and your sanctuary is primarily a place where you can let go of your obligations and be quiet, a haven that is deliberately low-maintenance, such as "The Tranquillity Garden" (page 78), will work best for you. Maintaining the garden should not become another chore on your "to do" list. Remember, too, as you consider the commitment the garden entails, that bigger is not nec-essarily better if you are unable to devote the time that proper maintenance requires. Most of the gardens pictured in this book can be recreated on a small scale; their details can also inspire a garden's design. Situating a bench near a simple but beautifully maintained, flourishing bed of scented flowers will do more to create sacred space out-doors than an ambitious garden layout that is poorly tended. Then, too, the lessons of spirit to be learned from gardening can be gleaned from "less" as easily as from "more," as a wonderful Zen anecdote told about the Japanese teahouse garden designer Riyku demonstrates. Riyku had grown a profusion of potted morning glories so beautiful and inspiring that talk of them reached the powerful provincial baron, who asked to come see them. When he arrived at the garden, the pots were empty, and the baron was furious. Profoundly insulted, he stormed into the teahouse where Riyku had arranged a single, per-fect morning glory. He had removed the others so that the flower's true and universal beauty could be perceived.

Remember that the feeling of spiritual connection to the garden depends upon feeling a part of the landscape. That connection can be achieved visually—by close observation of

the changes in the landscape—or through the work that is garden maintenance. These consistent, repetitive tasks act to slow us down and force us to pay attention to the details of our surroundings. Pinching back herbs, pruning weak or damaged branches, deadheading flowers to encourage their continued growth, raking and removing garden debris, and watering are all tasks that, in the spiritual garden, insinuate and involve us in the larger patterns of nature. Once again consider the needs of the individual plants, shrubs, and trees you intend to place in your garden of spirit and your ability to participate in taking care of them.

After you have spent time observing the site of your potential sanctuary, with pencil and paper in hand begin to consider the more permanent elements of the garden you wish to incorporate. If you plan on including a water feature, think about the visual and symbolic prominence

you want to give it in the space. Do you intend it to be a focal point, or will it simply be a detail? Is a meditation path essential to your spiritual practice? Remember that creating a spiritual garden is a process. Like your own spiritual awareness, the garden will evolve over time, and the goal here is not to create a space that instantly satisfies your aesthetic sense but one that, like the evolution of spirit and emotion, will reveal itself over time. Leave room for the plants to grow and for you to change your mind about the placement of elements.

Above: *A beautifully laid path in a private Ohio garden.*

Right: *A water feature creates variety in the spiritual garden's landscape.*

Above right: *At the Hermitage of the Dayspring, a meditation path runs alongside a rock wall, creating a sense of wonder.*

Opposite: *Watering and other maintenance tasks are exercises in spirit.*

THE SANCTUARY LANDSCAPE

Your intended use of the spiritual garden—whether it is a corner of your property or the entire yard—should be the cornerstone of its design, dictating the choice and placement of "hardscape" elements, permanent features such as pathways, walls, fences,

Above: *A subtle, patterned stone pathway in the Maryland garden of designer Osamu Shimizu.*

dividers, arbors, trellises, statuary, and furniture, as well as trees and shrubs. In the spiritual garden these elements have both functional and symbolic significance which will, along with the permanent plantings, create the over-

all atmosphere of the sanctuary. Setting off your sacred space from the heavily traveled areas of your property will help make it a place of retreat; you may want to surround an area set aside for meditation or prayer with a hedge or create an arbor, a place of shelter that can also be used as a support for trailing vines or climbing

roses. Gates act as literal and symbolic places of transition, and can also be used to great effect to create a feeling of sanctuary. Alternatively you may want to be able to see the garden from inside the house to integrate the spiritual landscape fully into your everyday life; this would dictate a more open design. The decision is an entirely personal one. For many people

movement is an essential part of spiritual work, and creating a pathway—even one that doesn't go very far in actual footage—may enrich a spiritual garden by suggesting the path that is spiritual growth. It can be a path that is meant to be walked or one that simply directs the eye through the landscape.

Seating is also an important part of any garden devoted to contemplation and increasing awareness.

> All things are connected. Whatever befalls the earth befalls the sons of the earth.
>
> *Chief Seattle*

Benches and chairs act as markers, directing our attention to specific elements in the surroundings, such as the distant view of a "borrowed landscape," an inspiring piece of statuary, or the sculptural shape of a tree. Once again, how you intend to use the sanctuary space should dictate the choices you make about seating. If you envision the garden as a communal space, where family and friends will gather, add a table and chairs. A stone bench is both beautiful and symbolically appropriate but, since it will be difficult to move once in place, its site should be carefully chosen, offering a view of the sanctuary that will inspire in all seasons. Furniture made of wood offers not only flexibility in arrangement but a variety of styles, ranging from the rustic to the the formal.

visual interest and symbolic meaning. Depending on its size and location, a statue can be the focal point of the garden or a simple, inspirational detail. Any object with personal and spiritual resonance can be used to great effect in the spiritual garden. (For more see Resources, page 180.)

Incorporating statuary and artwork into the spiritual garden enriches its texture, adding both

Above: *A beautiful rock meditation path at the Zen Mountain Monastery in Mt. Tremper, New York.*

Right: *A stepping-stone path in a private garden.*

Pathways: Pathways in the garden can be permanent, made of brick or slate, of gravel or pebbles, or deliberately temporary, made of log rounds, gravel, or even pine needles. A grass path is beautiful but cannot bear heavy traffic, while a stepping stone path will slow the walker's pace and encourages contemplation and meditation. The

range in cost (from the most expensive, slate, to the least, pine needles or bark), difficulty of installation, and maintenance is considerable. The more elaborate the path—for example, a brick walkway laid in a basket-weave or herringbone pattern—the more difficult and costly the installation. Before installing any path, particularly a permanent one, once again consider how you intend to use it and what you want it to add to the garden. In addition to cost and maintenance, consider the color of the material you've chosen to create the path and how it will work in the landscape. Do you want to emphasize the path or do you want it to look naturalistic? The layout of the pathway will affect both how it looks in the landscape and how you end up using it. A straight path will direct the eye through the garden, while a meandering or curving one will allow you to take in different details each time you walk it. A circular path will make whatever it surrounds—a fountain, a tree, or a statue—the focal point of the sanctuary. If your land is graded, adding steps to the path will encourage contemplation, and permit a different vision of the landscape as the viewer's eye level changes.

Fences, Natural Dividers, and Gates: These are the frames that define the boundaries of the sanctuary; the degree to which they enclose the garden varies enormously depending on their materials. A brick wall, for example, not only sets the garden off from its surroundings but provides a visual backdrop for flowers and foliage. More open fencing, fashioned out of latticework, bamboo, or even widely spaced picket, permits one area of the garden to incorporate itself visually into another. You should consider both the style of fencing and the effect of your climate on the material of which it's made, as well as cost.

Trees and shrubs can function as natural dividers. Conifers such as Japanese yew (*Taxus cuspidata*) or American arborvitae (*Thuja occidentalis*) will, in time, provide a solid, living, low-maintenance backdrop for your sanctuary, while muffling noise and focusing your field of vision. Bamboo, on the other hand, is much more open; in addition to being symbolically important (it is an emblem of longevity and continuity), its slender stems and graceful leaves are easily swayed by breezes, adding movement and sound to the garden. (Keep in mind, though, that it is an invasive plant.)

Gates help delineate sacred space and encourage us to pause and take in the details of our surroundings. Like fences, gates can be solid—protective in spirit, acting to wall off the "outside"—or relatively transparent, providing a point of transition as well as a glimpse of the sanctuary itself. Once again, in addition to design, durability, and expense, consider the effect the gate you have chosen will have on how you feel when you enter the sanctuary garden.

CREATING A WATER FEATURE

Incorporating water into the spiritual garden—whether it is an elaborate fountain, the smallest of waterfalls, or a simple pond—enhances the sanctuary and gives it texture, adding shimmering reflections, a variety of sounds, and energy. The elixir of life, water has the ability to calm and soothe; its presence makes the garden a more welcoming place for all manner of living creatures. Only a few of us are lucky enough to have natural water features in our gardens but, thanks to modern materials, enriching the sanctuary garden by including a water feature is both easy to do and relatively inexpensive. The simplest water garden is a container filled with water; the only requirements are that the container be both waterproof and cold-hardy. Many people use half whiskey barrels but because the wood retains toxins, the barrels need to be sealed with a fiberglass-based glaze or lined with synthetic material. If you like, the barrel can be sunk into the ground: Begin by a digging a hole just slightly deeper than the barrel itself, and then filling in

any gaps between the edge of the hole and the barrel with dirt. Fill with water, and then wait 24 hours before proceeding so that the water warms to air temperature and the chlorine and other chemicals dissipate. Edge the barrel with flat stones to disguise its rim. You can include a waterspout or fountain, or you can add plants to make a true water garden. Oxgenating plants—such as parrot's feather, arrowhead, and waterweed—make a filtration system unnecessary; by adding a goldfish or two you can rid the standing water of mosquito larvae (as well as introducing symbols of life and energy). Include small water lilies, potted up in either plastic or terra cotta, as well as marginals—grasses, taros, and rushes—to make your water garden a miniature paradise.

On a grander scale, you can also incorporate an artifical pond into your spiritual garden simply by digging a hole and then fitting it with a liner specially made for this purpose, available at garden centers and through

Above: *A delicate water feature at a private garden in Ohio, designed by landscape architect David Slawson.*

Opposite: *The open design of the slatted gate in Tommy Simpson's garden invites the visitor into the sanctuary.*

water garden catalogues. If you want to include a fountain or waterfall within your pond, you will need to situate it near a source of electricity and include a pump, either a free-standing surface unit or a submersible one, to circulate the water. If you are planning to add fish such as koi to the pond, you will probably need a filtration system. The water gardening books listed in the Resources section (page 180) will

keep in mind that the simpler the shape, the easier it will be to dig.

First dig a two-inch trench outside the outline to mark the area, and then dig within it; depending on the plants you want to grow, the hole will be somewhere between 15 and 24 inches deep; the edges should slope gently, at a 20-degree angle. You can also build steps along the edges to hold pots. Use a plumb line to make sure the perimeter of the

pond is level, and smooth out the bottom.

Drape your liner loosely over the hole. The weight of the water will press it into place, but make sure that there is enough liner to get to the bottom. Weight the liner's edges with large rocks and fill slowly with water, four to five inches at a time, allowing the water to settle before continuing. Fill to the top.

The pond can be edged naturalistically, using rocks of different shapes and sizes, or can be finished with brick or concrete.

The plants in the larger water garden will, like those in a smaller container, be kept in pots, and can include oxygenating plants that clean the water; marginal plants to add height and visual interest; floating plants such as duckweed to lend texture to the water's surface; and, of course, the stars of any water garden, water lilies and lotuses. Literally hundreds of cultivars are available, in a variety of colors and sizes. Among the most spiritual of all flowers, water lilies add an important dimension to any spiritual sanctuary.

give you step-by-step instructions, but basically you will need to do the following:

Choose a site for your pond; since most water plants require full sun, sunnier is better.

Design the pond's shape, and then mark it with chalk or strings and stakes. You can shape it naturally or choose a symbolic shape, but

Left and far left: *Water features add spirit to the garden and can be designed in different ways.*

Opposite: *What is more beautiful: the perfect leaf or the web of life?*

ORGANIC GARDENING

Organic gardening—cultivating without pesticides and chemicals—is part of spiritual commitment; responsible stewardship requires that we do as little as possible to disturb the web of life in our gardens. Gardening for the soul asks as well that we modify the competitiveness and perfectionism that may mark the rest of our lives and learn to work instead within meaningful boundaries. While each of us will want our spiritual garden to be lush and beautiful, there is an important lesson of spirit involved in recognizing that the unchecked pursuit of growing the "best" vegetables or the "biggest" blooms is not necessarily soul-serving. Gardening also teaches us the humility that is born of understanding the limits of control; everything we plant is subject to the larger cycles of nature. Finally remember that perfection in the spiritual garden isn't achieved in the perfect blossom or fruit but in the sustenance of a balanced ecosystem that nurtures all the garden's denizens. Practicing organic gardening helps us see the landscape holistically, and connects us, intellectually and spiritually, to the patterns of nature.

Integrating the principles of organic gardening into your private sanctuary isn't difficult; it simply

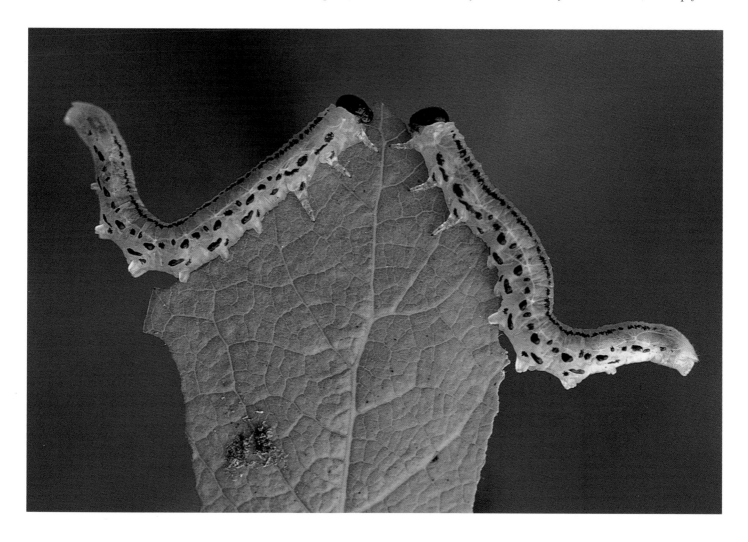

takes a certain amount of mindfulness, and you will be well rewarded for the effort. There are a few simple guidelines you will want to follow:

Bring understanding into your planning of the garden. If you choose plants that aren't appropriate for their location, they will not thrive, no matter what you do. An unhappy plant is more susceptible to disease and pest infestation. Be realistic about your choices, and pay attention to the amount of sun, water, and nutrients each plant needs before you plant. Remember, too, that plants need space to thrive. Don't succumb to the temptation of making the garden look fuller by planting too close together; be patient. Proper maintenance is the key to the health of any garden. Weed and water regularly.

Above: *A compost pile or bin imitates the natural cycle, using decomposed material to sustain new growth.*

Feed the soil and the soil will feed the plants, and the plants will feed your soul. Remember that soil is living, not inert—teeming with earthworms, bacteria, and organic matter. While some soils are naturally rich in nutrients most will have to be amended, by the addition of organic material. In nature, plants in the forest are fed by the cycle of life and death, the decomposing plant matter on the forest floor; in the garden, we can imitate this cycle by composting, retrieving garden debris—fallen leaves, grass clippings, and spent flowers—and mixing them with kitchen waste such as eggshells, coffee grounds, and potato peels, and then letting it all decompose in a corner of the yard or in any of the compost bins manufactured for the purpose. Spread over your garden beds, compost will improve drainage and give the soil the nutrients the plants need. In addition to providing the "black gold" expert gardeners swear by, composting has the added benefit of letting us participate actively in the continuing cycle of life.

Other soil amendments—fish emulsion, blood meal, well-rotted manure, kelp, ground-up seashells, and other products—can be used to enrich the soil of the garden as well. If you wish you can have your garden soil tested at a laboratory or your local co-op extension to find out what specific nutrients it needs. (For more, see Resources, page 180.)

Organic matter can be integrated into the soil by mulching, covering the soil with a layer of organic material such as shredded bark or pine needles. In addition, mulch eliminates weeds and shades the plant's roots, cutting down on the need for watering. At the end of the season turn the mulch down into the soil and allow it to decompose.

Make peace with pests by understanding that you will never be rid of bugs in the garden (nor, upon reflection, would you want to because pesticides kill beneficial and destructive insects without discrimination). Remember that you share your garden with literally millions of other living beings, some of which are invisible to the eye.

I have great faith in a seed. Convince me that you have a seed there and I am prepared to expect wonders.

Henry David Thoreau

IPM—Integrated Pest Management—is the responsible gardener's answer to the problem of pests. If you have planted with understanding—choosing the right plants for the soil and other conditions—and you are following a routine of maintenance, you are less likely to be invaded. Horticultural oils, which prevent mildew and make leaves unattractive to most pests, can also be used.

Practice crop rotation. This ancient practice not only helps the soil from being depleted of nutrients, but also thwarts the insects who have overwintered in the soil, waiting patiently for you to plant their favorite crop. Rotate beans and peas, for example, with tomatoes and eggplants. Companion planting, too, can help to keep plants strong and repel insects; for example, when basil and tomatoes are planted together, the basil repels the insects that feed on tomatoes. Planted near roses, garlic helps prevent blackspot, while chives planted nearby improve the growth and taste of carrots.

Monitor daily, particularly if you are growing vegetables (bugs find them as tasty as we do!); you can pick off the first of the invaders by hand and slow their population growth. Minor infestations can be stopped with a spray of water or water mixed with a little soap.

Use traps and barriers. A saucerful of beer is a magnet for slugs and snails, as is a piece of wood. (The snails hide underneath it and you can simply relocate them somewhere other than your sanctuary.) Diatomaceous earth—a sharp, fine-grained material that injures the bugs as they crawl over it—can also be sprinkled over the soil to deter pests; it is not harmful to earthworms, birds, or household pets.

Nature has its own system of checks and balances, and each garden pest has a predator in nature. While widespread use of pesticides has, unfortunately, reduced the population of "beneficial insects" and other predators, they can be imported into the sanctuary garden or lured there, by planting with them in mind. Ladybugs make a feast of 40 or so different kinds of insects, while wasps limit their intake to moth larvae. Toads, on the other hand, like dining on cutworms, caterpillars, and squash bugs, as long as you give them the habitat they need. Remember, though, that some beneficial insects—such as the praying mantis—eat both pests and other beneficial insects, and therefore should be introduced into the garden with caution.

Finally, if you must, you can also seek recourse to non-chemical, plant-based controls—products such as pyrethrin, neem, and garlic sprays—but keep in mind that these compounds are poisonous and can be every bit as dangerous as chemicals if they are used irresponsibly.

SEED-SAVING AND PROPAGATION

While most of us are used to getting our seeds in those pretty little packages with a picture of a perfect flower beaming out at us, we can move one step closer to nature by harvesting seeds from either our own plants or those of friends and acquaintances. The spiritual resonance of this particular kind of harvest is clear, but so are the pleasure and sense of accomplishment if offers, not unlike the satisfaction of baking from scratch rather than using a prepackaged mix. In some plants gathering the seed is easy: the cleome, for example, has hard-to-miss pods hanging from its stems while the pumpkin's seeds are part of the stringy inside you scoop out to make a jack-o'-lantern. The seeds of cosmos, black-eyed Susan, morning glory,

impatiens, and marigold are found in the seed head that forms at the center of the flower; harvest the head when it's ready to fall off of its own accord. Separate the seeds from the chaff and then dry them thoroughly. Seeds can be stored in the refrigerator in marked envelopes within an airtight container until you're ready to use them.

Most common plants germinate easily, if provided with the right conditions. Some large, hard seeds—such as morning glory, beans, and peas—will benefit from an overnight soaking in warm water. Because they have less complicated root systems, annuals are easier to germinate than perennials; a number of trees and shrubs require more complicated treatment to break dormancy.

The seeds you've saved can be sown directly in the ground when weather conditions are right, either in rows or, in imitation of the ways of nature, by scattering or broadcasting. (You'll lose some this way to birds and to the wind, but they will end up exactly where nature wants

Left: *The sight of a butterfly lighting on a flower, here a butterfly bush* (**Buddleia davidii**) *gladdens the heart and soul.*

Opposite: *Love-in-a-mist* (**Nigella damescena**) *has a special kind of beauty, intensified by its attractiveness to butterflies.*

them!) The seeds can also be started indoors and then, as seedlings, transplanted into the garden. For the majority of plants you can follow these simple steps:

Use a sterilized growing medium; you can buy packaged seed-starting soil or mix your own.

Use peat pots (best for fragile plants that don't like their roots disturbed, since the whole pot gets planted into the garden), store-bought flats, or even homemade containers (try egg or milk cartons) you've altered to create good drainage. Sow the seeds in rows or scatter them thinly and cover them with a small amount of soil, roughly equal to the thickness of the seed. Mist with water and then cover with plastic; at the first sign of germination remove the plastic.

Consult a good gardening book (see Resources, page 180) for information on the conditions required for germinating specific seeds. (Some need light to germinate, others darkness.)

After germinating, the seedlings need warmth (a temperature between 60 and 75 degrees Fahrenheit) and light. A sunny windowsill will do for starting seeds but, since the seedlings will orient themselves to any available light, they will become leggy and weak if the source of light isn't strong and consistent. A simple grow light will do the trick. Keep the seedlings well-watered but don't let the soil get soggy. Thin for both weakness and overcrowding; if the seedlings roots don't have enough room, transplant. When weather permits, take the seedlings outdoors in stages, getting them acclimatated to the outdoors (or "hardening them off" as the practice is known) and plant them in properly prepared soil.

The simple act of harvesting the seed at the dying-off of the flower and then planting the following spring roots us and our gardens in an eternal cycle; we are both the beneficiaries of and participants in an ongoing pattern of renewal, which informs our spirits as it clothes the earth with beauty.

BUTTERFLY GARDENING

Your spiritual garden can also be designed to attract butterflies and moths. In addition to being an ancient symbol of metamorphosis and resurrection, the butterfly—in cultures all over the world— is a potent emblem of the soul, and there is no sight as fitting to the mood of the spiritual garden as that of a beautiful butterfly lighting upon a flower. In ancient Greek art the soul was depicted as leaving the body in the form of a butterfly; among the Aztecs butterflies hovering above flowers signified the presence of the souls of fallen war-

Yellow butterflies
Over the blossoming,
virgin corn,
With pollen-spotted
faces
Chase one another in
brilliant throng.

Hopi, "Kachina Song"

riors. In Christian art Christ is often pictured with a butterfly in hand, symbolic of the Resurrection. Planting for these winged creatures teaches an important lesson in stewardship: the increasing loss of natural habitats— fields and meadows turned into highways and manicured lawns inhospitable to butterflies—has, not surprisingly, resulted in a loss of native species, some of which require a single

host plant for the larval stage of their lives. The monarch, for example, depends on milkweed; without it the population declines and finally disappears from an area. Planting wildlfowers native to your area is an important step in sustaining this beautiful and inspirational form of wildlife and, once again, acknowledging the web of life in the spiritual garden.

You can plan an entire garden to attract butterflies, or you can designate a single bed or corner by planting with them in mind. Remember that the cold-blooded butterfly needs sunlight to warm its muscles and undisturbed space to browse from flower to flower for nectar. It will also need a source of water; if you have a birdbath, simply put a stone or two in it, since the butterfly needs to be above the

Above: *In addition to its powerful spiritual symbolism, the peony will also attract butterflies into the sanctuary garden.*

Opposite: *The simplest of indoor sanctuaries: an exquisite orchid frames a statue of Buddha on a tabletop, creating sacred space.*

waterline to sip. If you are planning a water feature or pond, all the better. The area you choose for your butterfly garden should also offer some protection from the wind through the means of a fence, wall, or shrubbery. As Melody Mackey Allen advises in the useful book *Butterfly Gardening*, you can plant shrubs that do the work of both attracting and protecting these winged visitors, such as glossy abelia and wax-leaf privet.

SPIRITUAL GARDENING INDOORS

The spiritual lessons of the garden can be part of our daily lives even in those seasons when the outdoor garden has to be abandoned. Indoor gardening can be as simple or as ambitious as you wish; the mindfulness that spiritual gardening induces has little to do with scale. Even a simple pot of ivy (*Hedera helix*), easy to care for and simple to root in water, can become an indoor garden of spirit; ivy is an ancient emblem of the life force, an attribute of many of the gods of resurrection, and thus a reminder that the seasonal cycle is never static.

Scent and color are powerful reminders of the beauty and the spirit inherent in the natural world, even when the trees are bare and the sky is gray. Forcing bulbs, corms, and pips, as well as the branches of both flowering and nonflowering trees, can be part of a spiritual exercise that keeps our hearts and spirits open, even during those months of the year when the soul food nature provides seems to be largely absent. Among the bulbs you may want to use for your indoor garden of spirit are the crocus, the sweet paperwhite, the perfumed and colorful hyacinth, the stately and elegant lily, and the delicate and scented lily of the valley. Their sacred stories help to enliven the heart in the season of retreat.

The crocus is a member of the distinguished iris family (Iridaceae) , and among its species is the saffron crocus (*Crocus sativus*), which was sacred to the Greeks and ancient Hebrews. The hyacinth (*Hyacinthus orientalis*) was held to be sacred to the Greek goddess of agriculture, Ceres, and it may, according to some experts, be the "lily" referred to in the Song of Solomon (6:2–4) since it is native to the northern areas of the Middle East, including the hills of Galilee. In the Christian tradition the hyacinth symbolizes the peace of a mind focused on heaven. The paperwhite (*Narcissus tazetta*) too has a sacral history: It may well be the "rose of Sharon" referred to in the Song of Solomon, since it blooms in profusion on the plain of Sharon at the beginning of the winter rainy season. While it is now primarily associated

> Arranging a bowl of flowers in the morning can give a sense of quiet in a crowded day—like writing a poem or saying a prayer.
>
> *Anne Morrow Lindbergh*

with Easter, the Madonna or white lily (*Lilium candidum*) was a symbol of motherhood in Semitic culture, thus became associated with the Virgin Mary. In Christian flower legend the lily-of-the-valley (*Convallaria* sp.) was an emblem of Christ's Second Coming; one of its common names, "Mary's tears," derives from the legend that the flowers sprung from Mary's tears at the Crucifixion.

Forcing the branches of deciduous trees and shrubs is a different kind of spiritual exercise. Ancient fertility rites usually involved deciduous trees because their spring flowering and leafing-out symbolized resurrection, and many of the branches easily forced have sacred stories attached to them. If you are taking cuttings from your own trees and shrubs, remember that the later you harvest in the winter season, the quicker the bloom indoors. A clean 45-degree cut at the terminus of the branch is best; simply arrange the branches in a vase or container in clear, room-temperature water. Among the most beautiful branches to force are witch hazel (*Hamamellis* sp.) and winter hazel (*Corylopsis pauciflora*), sacred to the Celts. Flowering almond (*Prunus triloba*) has small, pink double flowers; because it is one of the first trees to flower, it symbolizes rebirth in the Hebrew tradition (although, because of its susceptibility to late frosts, it is also a symbol of transience). Try forcing flowering cherry (*Prunus sargentii*) or dogwood (*Cornus mas* or *Cornus florida*). Forcing branches indoors and watching the buds change and then finally unfurl into blossom is both life-affirming and soul-strengthening.

Sources

PLEASE NOTE: these listings are provided for the convenience of the reader and do not constitute a recommendation by the author.

PLANTS, BULBS, AND SEEDS

Abundant Life Seed Foundation
P. O. Box 772
Port Townsend, WA 98368
Telephone: (360) 385-566.

Bamboo Sourcery
666 Wagnon Road
Sebastopol, CA 95472.
Open by appointment only.
Telephone: (707) 823-5866
Website: www.bamboo.nu
Over 200 different species of bamboo; demonstration gardens

Dabney Herbs
P.O. Box 22061
Louisville, KY 40252
Telephone: (502) 893-5198
Quality herbs, plants, botanicals, essential oils, aromatherapy supplies, and books

The Daffodil Mart
30 Irene Street
Torrington, CT 06790
Telephone: (800) ALL-BULB
Supplier of bulbs

Dutch Gardens
P. O. Box 200
Adelphia, NJ 07710
Telephone: (800) 818-3861
Fax: (732) 780-7720
Bulbs and perennials

Heirloom Garden Seeds
P.O. Box 138
Guerneville, CA 95446

Heirloom Old Garden Roses
24062 NE Riverside Drive SG,
St. Paul, OR 97137
Telephone: (503) 538-1576

Kurt Bluemel, Inc.
2740 Greene Lane
Baldwin, MD 21013
Telephone: (410) 557-7229
Fax: (410) 557-9785
Bamboo, grasses, and perennials

Niche Gardens
1111 Dawson Road
Chapel Hill, NC 27516
Telephone: (919) 967-0078
Website: www.nichegdn.com.
Native Southeastern plants as well as ornamental grasses and perennials

Old House Gardens
536 Third Street
Ann Arbor, MI 48103
Telephone: (734) 995-1486
Fax: (734) 995-1687
Website: www.oldhousegardens.com
Heirloom bulbs

Prairie Nursery, Inc.
P. O. Box 306
Westfield, WI 53964.
Telephone: 800-476-9453
In Canada: 888-476-7303
Fax: 608-296-2741
Website: www.prairienursery.com.
Wildflowers, native grasses, plants, and seeds; meadow design

Seed Savers Exchange
Route 3, Box 239
Decorah, IA 52101

Seeds of Change
1364 Rufino Circle #5
Sante Fe, NM 87501
Telephone: (505) 438-8080
Heirloom and open-pollinated seeds

Siskiyou Rare Plant Nursery
2825 Cummings Road
Medford, OR 97501
Telephone: (541) 772-6846
Japanese maples and conifers.

Slocum Water Gardens
1101 Cypress Gardens Boulevard,
Winter Haven, FL 33884
Telephone: (941) 293-7151
*Aquatic plants and marginals, all
water garden supplies*

Southern Exposure Seed Exchange
P.O. Box 170
Earlysville, VA 22936
Telephone: (804) 973-4703
Heirloom and open-pollinated seeds

Tripple Brook Farm
37 Middle Road
Southampton, MA 01073
Telephone: (413) 527-4626
Website: www.tripplebrookfarm.com
*Native Northeastern plants, including
acquatics and marginals*

**Van Bourgondien Bulbs and
Perennials**
P. O. Box 1000-4781
Babylon, NY 11702
Telephone: (800) 622-9997

LANDSCAPE DESIGN AND CONSULTATION

Marty Cain
55 Park Street
Newport, NH 03773
Telephone: (603) 863-7343
e-mail: marty@sugar-river. net
Labryinth design

Dr. Alex Champion, Earth Symbols
P.O. Box 145
Philo, CA 95466
Fax: (707) 895-2598
e-mail: champion@zapcom. net
Website: www. earthsymbols. com
*Creation of rock and earthworks
based in sacred geometry*

Thomas Batcheller Cox
101 South Madison Avenue
Pasadena, CA 91101
Telephone: 626-792-9222

Chris Jacobson, GARDENART
P.O. Box 494
Los Gatos, CA 95031
Telephone: (415) 564-5913
Website: www.gardenart.to
Ecology-conscious garden design

The Labyrinth Society
P.O. Box 144
New Canaan, CT 06840
Telephone: (877) 446-4520
*A global organization devoted to sup-
porting those who create, use, and
maintain labyrinths*

LANDGARDEN Landscape
Architects,215 Park Avenue South,
New York, New York 10003
(212) 228-9500
Design of residences and public space

Jeff Lee/Lee & Liu Associates, Inc.
638 I St NW
Washington, DC 20001
Telephone: (202) 466-6666

Jami Lin, Earth Design Inc.
P.O. Box 530725
Miami Shores, FL 33153
Telephone: (305) 756-6426
Website: www.netrun-
ner.net/~earthdes/
Feng Shui consultant

Mark Leuchten, Wind Water Designs
40 Maple Street
Princeton, NJ 08542
Telephone: (609) 497-4883
Feng shui landscaping

J. Mendoza, Gardens, Inc.
18 West 27th Street
New York, NY 10001 Telephone:
Telephone: (212) 686-6721
*Design and installation of both city
and country garden designs*

**Stephen Morrell, Contemplative
Landscapes**
57 Cedar Lake Road
Chester, CT 06412
*Public and private gardens; Zen prac-
titioner*

Shinichiro Abe/ZEN Associates
124 Boston Post Road
Sudbury, MA 01776
Telephone: 978 443-6222
http://www.zenassociates.com

Osamu Shimizu, Shimizu Landscape Corporation
6101 Bryn Mawr Avenue
Glen Echo, MD 20812
Telephone: (301) 229-9483.
Interpretation of Eastern elements in Western gardens

David Slawson
Cleveland, Ohio
Telephone: (216) 520-6331
Specializes in Japanese-style gardens

Jaen Treesinger
P.O. Box 867
Mendecino, CA 95460.
Telephone: (707) 937-1856
e-mail: treesong@ mcn.org
Horticulturalist and garden designer

Takeo Uesugi, TUA, Inc.
3434 Holt Avenue
West Covina, CA 91791
Telephone: (626) 331-8066
e-mail: Tuainc@worldnet.att.net

Pamela Woods, Sacred Gardens
Based in the United Kingdom
Telephone: 01453-885903
Spiritual garden design

GARDEN ACCESSORIES

Bamboo Fences
31 Germania Court
Jamaica Plains, MA 02130
Telephone: (617) 524-6137
Fax: (617) 524-6100
Bamboo furniture, fences, trellises

Bridgeworks
432 North Columbia Street
Covington, LA 70433
Telephone: (504) 893-7933
Japanese-style bridges

Cherry Blossom Gardens
15709 N. Lund Road
Eden Prairie, MN 55346
Telephone: (612) 975-0976
water basins, lanterns, bamboo, stepping stones, etc.

Dalton Pavilions
20 Commerce Drive
Telford, PA 18969
Telephone: (215) 721-1492
Fax: (215) 721-1501
Red cedar gazebos, pergolas, architectural birdhouses, and pagodas

DharmaCrafts
405 Waltham Street, Suite 234
Lexington, MA 02173
Telephone (781) 862-9211
Fax: (781) 862-8884
Buddhist meditation supplies, including stauary, gongs, and bells

Feng Shui Warehouse
P. O. BOX 6689
San Diego, CA 92166
Telephone: (800) 399-1599
Fax: (800) 997-9831.
Crystals, wind chimes, fountains, and more from this catalogue source

Gone with the Wind Chimes
7609 New Utrecht Avenue
Brooklyn, NY 11214
Telephone: (718) 256-8773
Fax: (718) 233-8054
Feng shui products including windchimes, crystals, mirrors, and books

Kenneth Lynch & Sons
84 Danbury Road
P.O. Box 488
Wilton, CT 06897
Telephone: (203) 762-8363
Fax: (203) 762-2999
Website: www.klynchandsons.com
Bird baths, benchs, fountains, sundials, statuary, including many saints

Lilypons Watergardens
P.O. Box 14
Buckeyestown, MD 21717
Telephone: (800) 723-7667 or
P.O. Box 188
Brookshire, TX 77423
Telephone: (800) 765-5459; or
P.O. Box 1130
Thermal, CA 92274
Telephone: (800) 365-5459.
Complete water garden supplies

Nampara Gardens
P. O. Box 652
Trinidad, CA 95570
Telephone: (707) 677-3567
*Redwood bridges, lanterns, gates,
benches*

The Nature Company
P. O. Box 188
Florence, KY 41022
Telephone: (800) 227-1114

Natural Wonders®
Telephone: (800)-2WONDER
Website: www.naturalwonders.com
*Unique items inspired by nature for
the garden*

Rising Sun Gardens
4451 Rte 27
Princeton, NJ 08540
Telephone: (609) 924-2743
*Carved granite and marble, lanterns,
bowls and bridges*

Sacred Source
P.O. Box 163
Crozet, VA 22932
Telephone: (800) 290-6203
Fax: (804) 823-7665.
*Statuary for indoors and out from
spiritual traditions all over the world,
from paganism to Christianity,
Hinduism, and Buddhism*

Stone Forest
213 S. St. Francis Drive
Santa Fe, New Mexico 87501
Telephone: (505) 986-8883
Fax: (505) 982-2712
Website: www.stoneforest.com
*Fountains, functional sculpture, stone
lanterns, and basins for the Zen gar-
den or any garden of spirit*

Stonewoods Gallery
P.O. Box 35
Tuxedo, NY 10987
Telephone: (800) 786-6308
Fax: (800) 786-6361
*Inscribed natural river stones and
marble*

Tom Torrens Sculpture Design
P.O. Box 1819
Gig Harbor, WA 98335
Telephone: (253) 857-5831
Fax: (253) 265-2404
e-mail: tomtorrens@tomtorrens.com
Lanterns, gongs, bells, and fountains

Van Ness Watergardens
2460 N. Euclid Avenue
Upland, CA 91784
Telephone: (909) 982-2425,

The Waterworks
111 East Fairmont Street
Coopersburg, PA 18036
Telephone: 800-360-LILY.
*Pumps, fountains, linings, filtration
systems, and everything else for a
watergarden, including plants.*

Public Gardens to Visit

Asticou Azalea Gardens
Asticou Way, Mount Desert Island
Northeast Harbor, ME 04662
Japanese garden

Avena Botanicals
219 Mill St.
Rockport ME 04856
Telephone: (207) 594-0694
e-mail: avena@avenaherbs.com
Healing and aromatherapy gardens

Cathedral of St. John the Divine
Amsterdam Avenue and
112th Street
New York, NY 10025
Telephone: (212) 316-7540
Biblical garden

Chanticleer
786 Church Road
Wayne, PA 19087
Telephone: (610) 687-4163
Tranquility and water gardens

Chelsea Physic Garden
66 Royal Hospital Road
London England SW3 4HS
Telephone: (0171) 352 5646
Fax: (0171) 376 3910

Cleveland Botanical Garden
11030 East Boulevard
Cleveland, OH 44106
Telephone: (216) 721-1600
Japanese garden

Dayspring
Kent, Connecticut
Telephone: (860) 354-8727
e-mail: dayspringosb@snet.net

Filoli Gardens
Canada Road, off Highway 280
Woodside, CA 94062
Telephone: 650-364-8300
Formal and natural gardens

Green Gulch Farm Zen Center
1601 Shoreline Highway
Sausalito, CA 94965
Telephone: (415) 383-3134
Fax: (415) 383-3128

Hakone Japanese Gardens
2100 Big Basin Way
Saratoga, CA 95070
Telephone: (408) 741-4994
Website: www.hakonegardens.com

Lillian Holt Center for the Arts
102 McCormick Avenue
Baltimore, MD 21206
Telephone: (410) 882-6002
Labyrinth of ornamental grasses

The John P. Hume Japanese Stroll Garden
Dogwood Lane
Mill Neck, New York 11756
Telephone: (516) 674-3168

The Institute for American Indian Studies
38 Curtis Road, Box 1260
Washington, Connecticut 06793
Telephone: (860) 868-0518
Fax: (860) 868-1649
Medicine wheel garden

The Japanese Garden of Portland, Oregon
611 SW Kingston Avenue
Portland, Oregon 97208
Telephone: (503) 223-1321

Mount Calvary Retreat House
P.O Box 1296
Santa Barbara, California 93102
Telephone: (805) 962-9855 ext. 10
Meditation garden

Mount Manresa Jesuit Retreat
239 Fingerboard Road
Staten Island, NY.10305
Telephone: (718) 727-3844
Meditation garden, Mary garden

Neot Kedumim Biblical Preserve
Route 443
Israel
Telephone: (972) 8-977-0777.
Fax: (972) 8-977-0766

Nitobe Garden
University of British Columbia
Vancouver, British Columbia, Canada
Telephone: (604) 822-0666
Japanese garden

Rodef Shalom Biblical Botanical Garden
4905 Fifth Avenue
Pittsburgh, PA 15213
Telephone: (412) 621-6566

Seiwan-In
Missouri Botanical Garden
4344 Shaw Road
St. Louis, MO 63110
Telephone: (800) 642-8824

Shoyoan Teien
Wesleyan University
343 Washington Terrace.
Middletown, Connecticut 06459
Telephone: 860-685-2000
Japanese garden

Rudolf Steiner Fellowship Foundation
Spring Valley, New York
Telephone: (914) 356-8984
Organic herb and healing gardens

Staten Island Botanical Garden
914 Richmond Avenue
Staten Island, NY
Telephone: (718) 273-8200
Chinese scholar's garden

Sun Yat Sen Classical Chinese Garden
578 Carrall Stret
Vancouver, British Columbia VB8 2J8
Telephone: (604) 689-7133

Tatton Park Japanese Gardens
Knutsford, Chesire, U .K.
Telephone: (0156) 565-4822

Warsaw Biblical Garden
Corner of Canal Street and SR15N,
Warsaw, IN, 46580
For more information, contact
Warsaw Community Development
Corporation, (800) 800-6090.

Zen Mountain House
Mt. Tremper, NY 12457
Tel. 1: (914) 688-2228
Fax: (914) 688-2415
e-mail: zmmtrain@zen-mtn.org

Selected Bibliography

Gardening for the Soul

Biedermann, Hans. *Dictionary of Symbolism.* Translated by James Hulbert. New York and Oxford: Facts on File Publishers, 1989.

Bowker, John, ed. *The Oxford Dictionary of World Religions.* New York and Oxford: Oxford University Press, 1997.

Budge, E. A. Wallis. *The Gods of the Egyptians; Studies in Egyptian Mythology.* New York: Dover Publications, 1969.

Campbell, Joseph. *The Mythic Image.* Princeton: Princeton University Press, 1974.

Chevalier, Jean and Alain Gheerbrant. *The Penguin Dictionary of Symbols.* Translated by John Buchanan-Brown. New York and London: Penguin Books, 1996.

Circlot, J. E. *A Dictionary of Symbols.* Translated by Jack Sage. New York: Philosophical Library, 1971.

Clarkson, Rosetta E. *Magic Gardens: A Modern Chronicle of Herbs and Savory Seeds* New York: The Macmillan Company, 1939.

Davidson, Georgie. *Classical Ikebana: the Art of Japanese Flower Arrangement.* South Brunswick and NY: A.S. Barnes and Company, 1970.

Druse, Ken. *The Shade Garden.* New York: Clarkson Potter, 1992

Erman, Adolph. *Life in Ancient Egypt.* New York: Dover Publications, 1971..

Goody, Jack. *The Culture of Flowers.* New York: Cambridge University Press, 1993.

Leach, Maria and Jerome Fried. *Funk and Wagnalls Standard Dictionary of Folklore, Mythology, and Legend.* San Francisco: HarperSanFrancisco, 1984.

McClure, Susan. *Rodale's Successful Organic Gardening; Companion Planting.* Emmaus, PA: Rodale Press, 1994.

Penney, John. *The Master's Book of Ikebana.* New York: The Two Continents Publishing Group, 1976.

Riotte, Louise. *Roses Love Garlic: Secrets of Companion Planting with Flowers.* Pownal, VT: Storey Communications, Inc., 1983.

Riotte, Louise. *Carrots Love Tomatoes: Secrets of Companion Planting for Successful Gardening.* Pownal, VT: Storey Coomunications, Inc., 1975.

Tresidder, Jack. *Dictionary of Symbols: an Illustrated Guide to Traditional Images, Icons, and Emblems.* San Francisco: Chronicle Books, 1997.

Whiteside, Katherine. *Classic Bulbs: Hidden Treaures for the Modern Garden.* New York: Villard Books, 1991.

Wilson, Edward O. *The Diversity of Life.* Cambridge, MA: The Belnap Press of Harvard University Press, 1992.

The Tranquillity Garden

Glattstein, Judy. *Waterscaping: Plants and Ideas for Natural and Created Water Gardens.* Pownal, VT: Storey Communications, 1994.

Paul, Anthony and Yvonne Rees. *The Water Garden.* New York: Penguin Books, 1986.

Tomocik, Joseph with Leslie Garisto. *Water Gardening.* New York: Pantheon Books, 1996.

The Healing Garden

Bremness, Lesley. *The Complete Book of Herbs: A Practical Guide to Growing and Using Herbs.* New York: Viking Studio, 1988.

Chevallier, Andrew. *The Encyclopedia of Medicinal Plants: A Practical Reference Guide to more than 550 Key Medicinal Plants and Their Uses.* New York: DK Publishing, 1996.

Duke, James A., Ph.D. *The Green Pharmacy: The Ultimate Cmpendium of Natural Remedies from the World's Foremost Authority on Healing Herbs.* New York: St. Martin's Press, 1997.

Miller, Amy Bess. *Shaker Herbs: A History and Compendium.* New York: Clarkson N. Potter, Inc., 1976.

Phillips, Rogers and Nicky Foy. *The Random House Book of Herbs.* New York: Random House, 1990.

The Zen Garden

Engel, David. *A Thousand Mountains, A Million Hills: Creating the Rock Work of Japanese Gardens.* Tokyo: Shufunotomo Japnaese Publications, 1994.

Fischer-Schreiber, Ingrid, Franz-Karl Ehrhard, and Michael S. Diener. *The Shambhala Dictitionary of Buddhism and Zen,* translated by Michael H. Kohn. Boston: Shambhala Publications, 1991.

Itoh, Teiji. *Space and Illusion in the Japanese Garden.* New York and Tokyo: Weatherhill/Tankosha, 1973.

Nitschkte, Gunter. *Japanese Gardens.* Cologne and New York: Benedikt Taschen Verlag, 1993.

The Japanese Garden Society of Oregon. *Oriental Gardening.* New York: Pantheon Books, 1996

Okakura, Kakuzo. *The Book of Tea.* New York: Dover Publications, 1964.

Oster, Maggie. *Reflections of the Spirit: Japanese Gardens in America.* New York: Dutton Studio Books, 1993.

Suzuki, Daisetz T. *Zen and Japanese Culture.* New York: MJF Books, n.d.

The Gaia Garden

Cox, Jeff. *Your Organic Garden.* Emmaus, PA: Rodale, 1994

Jabs, Carolyn. *The Heirloom Gardener.* San Francisco: Sierra Club Books, 1984.

Kavasch, E. Barrie. *Enduring Harvests: Native American Foods and Festivals for Every Season.* Old Saybrook, Connecticut: The Globe Pequot Press, 1995.

Kavasch, E. Barrie. *Native Harvests: American Indian Wild Foods and Recipes.* Washington, Connecticut: The Institute for American Indian Studies/Birdstone Publishers, 1998.

Reichard, Gladys A. *Navaho Religion: A Study of Symbolism.* Princeton: Princeton University Press, 1977.

Stein, Sara. *Noah's Garden: Restoring the Ecology of Our Own Backyards.* Boston and New York: Houghton Mifflin Company, 1993.

The Aromatherapy Garden

Ackerman, Diane. *A Natural History of the Senses.* New York: Random House, 1990

Verey, Rosemary. *The Scented Garden,* New York: Random House, 1981

Wilder, Louise Beebe. *The Fragrant Garden: A Book about Sweet Scented Flowers and Leaves.* New York: Dover Publications, 1974.

The Feng Shui Garden

Hale, Gill. *The Feng Shui Garden: Design your Garden for Health, Wealth, and Trappings.* Pownal, VT: Storey Books, 1998.

Kingston, Karen. *Creating Sacred Space with Feng Shui:Learn the Art of Space Clearing and Bring New Energy into Your Life.* New York: Broadway Books, 1997.

Lagatree, Kristen M. *Feng Shui: Arranging Your Home to Change Your Life.* New York: Villard Books, 1996.

Lin, Jami. *The Essence of Feng Shui: Balancing Your Body, Home, and Life with Fragrance.* Carlsbad, CA: Hay House, 1998.

Rossbach, Sarah. *Feng Shui: The Chinese Art of Placement.* New York: E.P. Dutton, 1983.

Spear, William. *Feng Shui Made Easy: Designing Your Life with the Ancient Art of Placement.* San Francisco: HarperSanFran-cisco, 1995.

Too, Lillian. *The Complete Illustrated Guide to Feng Shui for Gardens.* Boston: Element Books, 1998.

Williams, C.A.S. *Outlines of Chinese Symbolism and Art Motives.* New York: Dover Publications, 1976.

The Celtic Garden

Ellis, Peter Berresford. *The Druids.* Grand Rapids, MIL William B. Eerdmans Publishing Company, 1994.

Graves, Robert. *The White Goddess: A Historical Grammar of Poetic Myth.* New York: Farrar, Straus & Giroux, 1975.

Matthews, Caitlin and John. *The Encyclopaedia of Celtic Wisdom.* Rockport, MA: Element Books, 1994.

Pennick, Nigel. *The Celtic Cross: An Illustrated History and Celebration.* London: Blandford/Cassell, 1997.

The Bible Garden

Hareiuveni, Nogah. *Ecology in the Bible.* Neot Kedumim, Israel: Neot Kedumim, The Biblical Landscape Reserve,1997.

Hareiuveni, Nogah. *The Emblem of the State of Israel: Its Roots in the Nature and Heritage of Israel.* Translated by Helen Frenkley. Neot Kedumim, Israel: Neot Kedumim, The Biblical Landscape Reserve,1988.

Jacob, Irene. *Biblical Plants: A Guide to the Rodef Shaom Biblical Botanical Garden.* Pittsburgh: Rodel Shalom Press, 1989.

King, Eleanor Anthony. *Bible Plants for American gardens.* New York: Dover Publiactions, 1975 reprint.

Swenson, Allan A. *Your Biblical Garden: Plants of the Bible and How to Grow Them.* Garden City, New York: Doubleday & Company, Inc., 1981.

The Saint's Garden

Ferguson, George. *Signs and Symbols in Christian Art.* Oxford: Oxford University Press, 1971.

Gordon, Lesley. *Green Magic: Flowers, Plants, and Herbs in Lore and Legend.* New York: The Viking Press, 1971.

Xerces Society and the Smithsonian Institution. *Butterfly Gardening: Creating Summer Magic in Your Garden.* San Francisco: Sierra Clubs Books, 1990.

The Labryinth Garden

Artress, Dr. Lauren. *Walking a Sacred Path: Rediscovering the Labyrinth as a Spiritual Tool.* New York: Riverhead Books, 1995.

Champion, Alex. *Earth Mazes.* Albany, California: Earth Maze Publishing, 1990.

Gardening as a Spiritual Exercise

The American Garden Guides. New York: Pantheon Books, 1994-1997.

Bradley, Fern Marshall and Barbara W. Ellis. *All-New Encyclopedia of Organic Gardening.* Emmaus, PA; Rodale Press, 1992.

Brickel, Christopher, Elvin MacDonald, Trevor Cole, eds. *The American Horticultural Society Encyclopedia of Gardening.* New York: DK Publishing, 1993.

Bubel, Nancy. *The New Seed Starter's Handbook.* Emmaus, PA: Rodale Press, 1988.

Cathay, Dr. Marc with Linda Bellamy. *Heat Zone Gardening.* Alexandria, VA: Time Life Custom Publishing, 1998.

Clausen, Ruth Rogers and Nicholas H. Ekstrom. *Perennials for American Gardeners.* New York: Random House, 1989.

Damrosch, Barbara. *The Garden Primer.* New York: Workman Publishing, 1988.

Darke, Rick. *Color Encyclopedia of Ornamental Grasses: Sedges, Rushes, Restios, Cat-Tails, and Selected Bamboos.* Portland, Oregon: Timber Press, 1999.

Ellis, Barbara W. and Fern Marshall Bradley. *The Organic Gardner's Handbook of Natural Insect and Disease Control.* Emmaus,PA: Rodale Prss, 1990.

__*Time-Life How-To Gardening: Garden Designs.* Alexandria, Virginia: Time Life Custom Publishing, 1997.

—*Gardening Basics.* Alexandria, Virginia: Time Life Custom Publishing, 1997.

Wyman,. Donald. *Wyman's Gardening Encyclopedia,* 2nd edition. New York: Macmillan Publishing Company, 1987.

Further Reading (Also see Select Bibliography)

Hallam, Elizabeth. *Saints: Who They are and how they help you.* New York: Simon & Shuster, 1994.

Kavasch, E. Barrie and Karen Baar. *American Indian Healing Arts: Herbs, Rituals, and Remedies for Every Season of Life.* New York: Bantam Books, 1999.

Kelly, Jack and Marcia. *Sanctuaries, the Complete United States: A Guide to Lodging in Monasteries, Abbeys, and Retreats.* New York: Bell Tower, 1996.

__*The Whole Heaven Catalog: A Resource Guide to Products, Services, Arts. Crafts, & Festivals of Religious, Spiritual, and Cooperative Communities.* New York: Bell Tower, 1998.

Lawlor, Anthony. *A Home for the Soul: A Guide for Dwelling with Spirit and Imagination.* New York: Clarkson Potter Publishers, 1997.

Index

Boldface type refers to illustrations.

A

Abiding Peace Lutheran
Church, 117
Abundant Life Seed
Foundation, 114
Acer palmatum, 101
Achillea millefolium, **92**
Ackerman, Diane, 125
aconite, **92,** 94
acorns, 142
Adiantum pedatum, **26**
Adonis, 59
Agastache foeniculum, 126
Agave americana, **93**
AIDS, 90, 96
Akebia quinata, 87
Alchemilla mollis, 85, **155**
algae, 71
Algonquin (peoples), 72
Allen, Melody Mackey, 178
alleopathic plants, 64
Allium, 64, 126
Allium sativum, 95, **128**
almond, flowering, 179
aloe, 85
Aloe polyphlia, **162**
Aloe vera, 95
Aloysia triphylla, 126
altars, 71-72, 95
Alviano, 153
Ameratsu, 101
American arborvitae,
84, 170
American Association of
Horticultural Therapists,
24
Amon, 30
Anasazi, 162
Anemone blanda, **30,** 152
Anethum graveolens,
92, 95
angelica, **93,** 95
Angelica archangelica,
93, 95
animal guardians, 134
anise hyssop, 126
Annunciation, 152
Antony, Mark 123
Apache, 162
aphid, 66
Aphrodite, 28, 59
apple mint, 126
apple tree, 118, 141, 143
apple tree, symbolism,
23, **24**

apricot tree, 148
arbors, 84
aromatherapy, 124
aromatherapy gardens,
122-129
Artemis, 62
artemisia, 26, 33
Artemisia absinthium, **146**
Arthur, King, 143
Artress, Lauren, 52, 159
artwork, 169
Asclepius, 90, 154
ash tree, 62, 140, 142
Assumption, 152
Assurbanipal, 13
Asteraceae, 49
Asticou Garden, **100**
Astilbe rosea 'Peach
Blossom', 126
Atropa belladonna, 94
Aurelius, Marcus, 94
autumn crocus, 94
autumn plumbago, 26
Avalon, 143
axis mundi, 142
Ayers Rock (Australia), 76
Ayurveda, 93
Aztecs, 92, 93, 177

B

bacteria, 68
bael tree, 90
bagua, 134, **135,** 136
balance, 35
bamboo, 65, 171
barberry, 50, 153
basil, 40, 64
bayberry, 72
bee, symbolism of, 65
bee-balm, 65
beech, 120
benches, **105, 124,** 154
benches, meditation, **52,**
71, **80, 83,** 148, **152,** 161
beneficial insects, 65, 66,
175
Bengal quince, 90
Bennett, Robin Rose, 63
Berberis, 50, 153
Betaine, feast of, 141
Betula lenta, **140**
Bible Garden (Cathedral of
St. John the Divine), 146
Bible, 118
biblical gardens, 51, 144,
149

birch tree, 140, 141
birds, 153
birds, planting for, 38
birds, symbolism of, **67,** 147
black birch, **140**
Black Hat Sect (feng
shui), 134
black walnut, 64, 117
black-eyed Susan, 65
blue cohosh, 94
blue flag, **144, 148**
blue poppy, **15**
blue, symbolism of, 30
bluebell, 120
blue-purple aster, 26
Boaz, 149
bodhi tree, 62, 106
Bodhidharma, 108
borage, 91
Borago officinalis, 91
borrowed landscape, 107,
168
Boston ivy, 86
boxwood, 50
Brahma, 58
branches, forcing, 179
bridges, symbolism of, **104**
Brittany, 141
Browning, Elizabeth
Barrett, 151
Buddha, **10,** 11, 20, **21,** 22,
28, 58, 62, 76, 105, **111**
Buddhism, 20, 50, 58, 104
Buddhism, Tibetan, 37,
59, 76, 159
Buddhism, Zen, 81, 99,
106, 107, 108
buddleia, 118
Buddleia davidii, **176**
bulbs, forcing, 178
Burt, Christopher, 76
Burt, Cindy, 76
butterflies, 52, **67,** 118,
119, 153, 154
butterfly bush, **176**
butterfly gardening,
177-178
Butterfly Gardening, 178
Buxus, 50

C

cabbage white, 67
caduceus, 90
Caesar, Julius, 140
Cain, Marty, 160
cairn, prayer, 72

Calendula officinalis, 95
Calycanthus floridus, **129**
Camellia 'Nicky Crisp', **32**
Camellia x *Williamsii*
'Debby', **32**
Campanula medium, **155**
Campbell, Joseph, 20
camphor thyme, 127
Candlemas, 58, 152
Canterbury bells, **155**
caraway thyme, 127
Cardamine pratensis, 152
cardinal directions, 72, 132
cardinal-flower, 118
carp, **66**
Carson, Jo, 25
Carson, Rachel, 166
cattail, 118
cauldron, 140
*Caulophyllum
thalictroides*, 94
cedar, 62
cedar of Lebanon, **148,**
148
Celtic calendar, 141
Celtic cross, 51, 141, 148
Celtic gardens, 138-143
Celts, 179
Centaurea cyanus, 65
Centers for Disease
Control, 94
*Ceratostigma
plumbaginoides*, 26
Cercis chinensis, 101
Ceres, 179
Cerridwen, 140
Chaaenomeles japonica, 101
chakras, 93
Chamaemelum nobile, 127
chamomile, **90, 127,** 127,
148, 154
Chamomilla recutita, 94
Champion, Alex, 52, 158,
159, 162
Changing Woman (Native
American), 12
Chanticleer, 80
Chartres, 159
Cherokee corn field bean,
115
cherry tree (flowering),
101, 179
chi, 19, 132, 133, 136, 139
Chief Seattle, 168
Chilean crocus, 30, **31**

Chinese cosmology, 132
Chinese culture, 99
Chinese redbud, 101
Chinese Scholar's
Garden, **130**
Choate, Dr. Jennifer, 163
chrism, 39
Christ Church (Port
Republic, Maryland),
147-148
Christian art, 177
chrysanthemum, 61
*Chrysanthemum parthe-
nium* , **93,** 95
cinnamon fern, 49
circle, symbolism of,
48, 50
Clark, Rev. Diana, 160
Clematis virginiana, 152
Cleopatra, 95, 123
Cleveland Botanical
Garden, **101**
clover, 91, 143
Colchicum autumnale, 94
color symbolism, 26-35
color, use of in the
garden, 80, 136, 178
comfrey, 92
companion planting, 63-
65, 68, 175
Compass school (feng
shui), 134
compass, 134
compost, 174, **174**
coneflower, 118, 120
Confucius (statuary), 135
conifers, 84
Connla's well, 142
containers (for plants), 83
Contemplative Prayer, 81
Convallaria, 179
coreopsis, 153
Corey, Brenda, 51
coriander, 64, 148, 149
Coriandrum sativum, 64
corn, 92
cornflower, 65
Cornus alba 'Siberica', 86
Cornus florida, 101, 179
Cornus mas, 179
Corsican mint, 127
Corylopsis pauciflora. 179
cosmos, 153
cottage pink, 126
courtyard gardens, 99, 109

crane, symbolism of, **103**
Creator, 67
Cretan labyrinths, 159, 161, 162
crocus, 58, 178
Crocus sativus, 178
Crocus tomasinianus, **58**
crop rotation, 175
cross (religious symbol), **83**
Crucifixion, 179
Cuchulain, 139
Curry, Helen, 159-160
curry plant, 126
cypress, 62
Cypripedium, **155**

D

Daisen-in dry garden, 106
daisy, 49
dandelion, 64, 92, 149
Darke, Rick, 25, 44-45, 52
date palm, **147**, 149
Daughters of Mother Earth, 63
De materia medica, 93
Dead Sea, 149
Delaware (peoples), 72
delphinium, 26
Demeter, 12
Dennis, Christy, 161
design, vocabulary of, 25-26
Deuteronomy, Book of, 146
dewy path, 108
dianthus, 32
Dianthus plumarius, 126
diatomaceous earth, 175
Diboll, Neil, 116
Digitalis purpurea, 94
dill, **92**, 95, 149
Dioscorides, 93
dividers, 55
divination, 142
divining rods, 142
dogwood, 101, 179
doorways, 55
dowsing rods, 142
dragonfly, 67
Dragon's breath, 132
druids, 140, 141, 142, 143
Druids, The, 142
Druse, Ken, 69
dry garden, 99, 111
du Cane, Florence, 110
duckweed, 82
dwarf fothergilla, 44

E

Earth Mazes, 52
Earth Mother, 46, 113, 115, 117, 119, 119, 122, 163
Earth, the Temple, and the Gods, The, 159

earthworks, 72, 162
earthworm, 65
Ebers Papyrus, 93, 95
Ecclesiastes, Book of, 42
echinacea, 154
Echinacea purpurea, **93**, 95, 120, **128**
Echinops, 49
Eckhardt, Meister, 160
Ecology of the Bible, The, 147
Eden, 17, 145
Egypt, ancient, 13, 40, 50, 52, 57, 66, 90, 93, 95, 158
eight sacred symbols (of Buddhism), 50
elder tree, 142
elderberry, 118
elements, five, 47, 132, 134
Ellis, Peter Berresford, 142
Emerson, Ralph Waldo, 44
En Gedi, 149
enclosures, 152
energy, 35
English ivy, 84
Enoch, Bill, 162-163
Environmental Protection Agency, 117
Eshmumun, 90
essential oils, **94**, 124
Euphorbia marginata, 85
Exodus, Book of, 147
Ezekiel, Book of, 152

F

fairies, 139
fairy moss, 82
fairy rings, 139, **143**
feminine, divine, 113, 120
fences (see also gates), 55, 83, 84, 170-171
feng shui gardens, **71**, 130-137
feng shui, 19-20, 36, 70
ferns, 108
fertility goddess, 60
feverfew, **93**, 95, 95
Fiacre, St., 154
Ficus religiosa, 106
ficus tree, 136
fig tree, 51, 62, 148
filbert, 118
Filipendula ulmaria, 126
fire, symbolism of, 141
fish, 137, 148
fiveleaf akebia, 87
Flack, Audrey, 114, 119, 121
Flanaghan, Kristina, 169
floating plants, 172
floral fragrance, symbolism of, 123

flower symbolism, 57
focal points, 137
forget-me-not, 26, 57, 57
Fothergilla gardenii, 44
fountain grass, 37
fountains, **47, 85**, 148, 152
foxglove, 94
fragrance, 39-41
Fragrant Garden, The, 32
Francis of Assisi, Saint, 71, 153-154
French lavender, **128**, 128
French marigold, 63
frog, **66**
Frost, Robert, 65
fruit trees, 137
fruit trees, symbolism of, 147

G

Gabaldo, Maria, 24-25
Gaia gardens, 20, 112-121
Galanthus, **58**, 152
Galen, 93
Ganesa, 40
gardens, earliest, 12-13
garlic, 64, 95, 128149
garlic sprays, 175
Gatefosse, Rene, 124
gates (see also doorways; fences), 55, 104, 108, 152, 170-171, **172**
gates, symbolism of, **49, 52, 55**
gazing balls, 137
Ge, 113
Genesis, Book of, 17, 36, 37, 47, 145
Gerken, Mary, 117
German chamomile, 94
germinating seeds, 177
Gethsemane, garden of, 18, 145
gladiolus, **29**
Glastonbury, England, **17**
globe thistle, 49
Glover, John, 52
Goddess, **138**
Goddess garden, 119-120
goldenseal, 94
goldfish, 83
Gowans, Tessa, 114
Grace Cathedral (San Francisco), 159
grapevine, 61, 118, 148
grass, ornamental, 37
gravel, raked, **50**, 105, **107**, 111
Graves, Robert, 141

Greece, ancient, 13-15, 40, 90, 91, 177
Greek anemone, **30**, 152
Green Dragon Temple, **117**
Green Gulch Farm, **117**
Green Man, **138**
green, symbolism of, 27-28
ground elder, 120
growing media, 177
Gubbio, 153

H

Hakone Japanese Gardens **6, 102-103, 106**
Halesia diptera var. magniflora, 44
Halesia tetraptera, 44
Hall, Edward, 107
Hamamellis, 179
hardening-off, 177
Hareuveini, Nogah, 147
Hathor, 49, 62
hawthorn, 62, 142
hazel, 62, 72, 141, 142
healing garden, 88-97
healing herbs, 72, 137
healing plants, 116
healing rites, 119
healing, garden's role in, 24, 95
healing, holistic, 124
Heaton, James III, 71
Hebrew tradition, 179
Hedera helix, 84, 178
hedges, 83, 84
Heimbach, Paul, 148-149
Heine, Heinrich, 22
heirloom gardening, 114, 116, **117**
Helianthus annuus, 64
Helichrysum petiolatum, 126
Heliopolis, 40
heliotrope, 61, **128**
hellebore, **26**
Helleborus orientalis, 26
hemlock, 26
Hera, 30, 57
herbs, bitter, 149
herbs, medicinal, 93
Hermitage of the Dayspring (Kent, Connecticut), **90, 167**
Herodotus, 159
Hesperis matronalis, 126
'Hidcote' lavender, 128
Hinduism, 29, 58, 90, 95
Hippocrates, 89, 93
Hodson, Sonia, 162-163
holly, 120
holy waters, 142
holy wells, 139

honeysuckle, 62, 118, 153
Hopi, 65, 163, 177
Hopkins, Gerard Manley, 152
Hopper, Donna, 51
Horeb, 146
horticultural oils, 175
Horus, 57
hosta, 87
Hosta 'Golden Scepter', 33
Hosta plantaginea 'Sweet Susan', 126
household gods, 40
Hume Stroll Garden, **19, 98, 105**
hummingbirds, 117
Huyler, Stephen, 22, 23-25, 56, 138
hyacinth, 178-179
Hyacinthus orientalis, 178-179
Hydrastis canadensis, 94
Hypericum perforatum, 95
hyssop, 51, 148, 154
Hyssopus officinalis, 51
Ilex verticillata, 153

I

Immaculate Conception, 152
in and yo, 100, 109
Incas, 59, 61, 92
incense, 123
Indian tradition, 47
indoor gardening, 178-179
Institute for American Indian Studies, **11,** 71-72, 116, 120
Institute for Child and Adolescent Development, 96
intuitive feng shui, 133
IPM (Integrated Pest Management), 175
Ireland, labyrinths in, 163
Iridaceae, 178
iris, **57**, 61, 118
Iris douglasiana, **69**
Iris pseudacorus, **149**
Iris versicolor, **148**
Irish Tree Alphabet, 141
Iroquois, 72
Isaiah, Book of, 18
Ise (Japan), 101
Isis, 12, 62, 90
Israel, 149
ivy, 178

J

Jacobson, Chris, 56, 71, 117
Japan, 99
Japanese gardens, **47**, 105, 106, 107

Japanese maple, 101
Japanese quince, 101
Japanese red pine, 101
Japanese stroll garden, 107
Japanese yew, 84, 170
Jarmon, Derek, 96
jasmine, 62, 126
Jasminum officinalis, **61**
Jeremiah, Book of, **18**
Jesus Christ, 55, 61, 62, 83, 141, 147
jewelweed, 72
John, Book of, 55
Jordan River, 149
Joseph of Arimaethea, 17, 18
journey, philosophical concept of, 107
Judeo-Christian tradition, symbolism in, 55
Juglans nigra, 64
juniper, 148
Juno, 30

K
Kavasch, Barrie, 71-72, 90, 116
Keller, Helen, 124
Kelly, Jack, 77
Kelly, Marcia, 77
Kentucky coffee tree, 118
King Solomon's Temple, 147
Kipling, Rudyard, 127
Knossos, 159
knot garden, 50
knotwork, Celtic, 143
koan, 81, 107
koi, **66**
Kokushu, Daito, 99
Korean ambassador's garden (Washington, D.C.), **20, 108**
Krishna, 40
Kuan Yin, 76
Kuck, Loraine, 107
Kurutz, Dennis, 71

L
labrys, 159
labyrinths, **10, 11**, 51, 52, 158, **161**
labyrinth gardens, 156-63
Labyrinth Project of Connecticut, 159-160
Labyrinth Society, 159
ladder, symbolism of, 52
ladybug, 66
lady's mantle, 87
Lakota, 72
Lakshmi, 29, 90
lamb's ear, 26

Land Form school (feng shui), 133
LANDGARDEN, 109
lanterns, 108
Lao Tzu, 70, 71, 131
lares familiares, 40
lark, 153
laurel, 120
Lavandula angustifolia, 51, 127
Lavandula stoechas, **128, 128**
lavender, **41**, 51, **124**, 127, 128, 129
Lawton, Cynthia, 26
Lebanon Valley College, 121
Lee, Jeff, 108
leek, 148
lemon balm, 95
lemon thyme, 127
lemon verbena, 126
Leuchten, Mark, 132, 137
lichens, 108
light, 35-36, 77
lighting, 137
Lilium candidum, 152, 179
lily, 148
lily-of-the-valley, 179
Limanthes douglasii, **69**
Lin, Jami, 70, 71, 133, 134, 137
Lindbergh, Anne Morrow, 29, 179
liriope, 148
Lo Shu, 134
Longgood, William, 9, 66
Longview Gardens, 45, 117
Lonicera fragrantissima, 53
loosestrife, 65, 149
lotus, **19**, 28, 57, 58, 59, **60, 78, 79**, 110, 149, **149, 172**
lotus, blue, 57
lotus, white, 57
Lotusland (Santa Barbara, California), **78**
Lounsberry, Alice, 40
love-in-a-mist, 148, **177**
Lug, 139
Lukas, Karen, 55
Luo pan, 134
Lysimachia, 65

M
MacCumal, Fionn, 139, 142

MacGuill (Irish king), 142
Madonna lily, 152, 179
Magi, three, 39
magic square, 134
magnolia, **41**
maidenhair fern, **26**
maintenance, 137, 166, 167, 174
maintenance (as spiritual activity), 151
mallow, 149
Man in the Maze (Native American), 158
mandala, **39, 52**, 76, 81, 159
Moon Gate, **130**
maple, 64
marginal plants, 171
marigold, **68**
marjoram, 148
Martineau, James, 149
Mary Magdalene, 18
Mayans, 93
mazes, 52
Meconopsis betonicifolia, **15**
medicinal plants, 154
medicine wheel, **11**, 119
medicine wheel gardens, 71, 71, 116, **120**
meditation gardens, **83, 90**, 118, 136, 168
meditation paths, 118
meditation, 71, 81, 105, 151, 159
megaliths, 141
Melissa officinalis, 95
memento mori, 76
Mendoza, Jeff, 35
menorah, 147
Mentha, 126
Mentha x *piperita* 'Chocolate', 126
Mentha requienii, 127
Mentha spicata, 64
Mentha suaveolens, 126
Merton, Thomas, 79, 81
Mesopotamia, 13
Michael (archangel), 95
microorganisms, 68
Miland, Emil, 76-77
milkweed, 154, 178
millet, 153
Minoan civilization, 57, 159
mint, 36, 126, 148
Miscanthus sinensis 'Zebrinus', 37
monarch butterfly, 67, Monarda, 65

moon garden, 120
moon, planting by, 44
moon, symbolism of, 41-42, 139
morning glory, **110**
Morrell, Stephen, 100
Moses, 146, 147
moss, 71, 72, 80, 108
Mother Earth, 120
motion, symbolism of, 153
Mount Calvary (Santa Barbara, California), 83, **124, 152**
Mount Manresea Jesuit Retreat House (Staten Island, New York), **150**
Mount Meru, 104, 105
mountain silverbells, 44
movement, 36-37
movement, use of in the garden, 168
mulch, 174
'Munstead' lavender, 128
mustard seed, parable of, 147
Myosotis, 26
myrtle, 62, 149
Myrtus communis, 149
Mystical Islands of the Blessed, 105

N
nannyberry, **29**
Narcissus tazetta, 179
narcissus, 148
National Arboretum, 58
Native American tradition, 48, 63, 65, 71, 95, 116
Native American tradition, color symbolism in, 27
Native American tradition, perception of nature in, 18-19
Native American tradition, the tree in, 62
Native Harvests, 90
native plants, 116, 119
Natural History of the Senses, A, 125
Natural Shade Garden, The, 69
nature, sacrality of, 17-20
Navajos, 159
neem, 175
New Testament, 62, 145, 147
New Zealand flax, 120
Newman, Cardinal Henry, 152

Nicotiana alata, **128**
Nigella damescena, **177**
nigella, 149
Nitschke, Gunter, 105-106
Nymphaea caerulea, 57
Nymphaea lotus, 57
Nyro, Laura, 21

O
oak, 62, 120, 140, 142
Ocimum basilicum, 64
ogham, 140
Old Testament, 62, 145, 149
omphalos, **157**
onion, 126
opium poppy, 94
orange, symbolism of, 29
oregano, 40, **128**
organic gardening, 69, 173-174
organic material, 174
Oriental garden, 10, 11
Origanum vulgare, 128
Osiris, 12, 28, 52, 57, 62
Osler, Mirabel, 75
Osmunda cinnamomea, 49
Oster, Maggie, 69, 110
Our Lady's mantle, **155**
Our Lady's slipper, **155**
Our Lady's smock, 152
oxygenating plants, 171

P
pa kua, 134
Paeonia, 94
Painswick Abbey, 58
Paleolithic era, 158
pampas grass, **35**
Panicum virgatum, 45
Papaver somniferum, 94
paperwhite, 179
papyrus, **144**, 148, 149
parrot's feather, 82
Parthenocissus tricuspidata, 86-87
Passion (of Christ), 152
passionflower, 154
Passover Seder, 149
paths (see also walkways), 47, 51, 52, 52, 80, 81, 82, **101**, 104, 108, 120, **122, 128**, 157, **159, 167, 168, 168, 169, 169**, 170
paths, meditation, 167, 169
patterns, 52
peace pole, 72
pear tree (flowering), 101
pear tree, 118
peat pots, 177
Pennisetum alopecuroides, 37

peony, **59**, 94
Perovskia atriplicifolia, 126, 128
pesticides, 70, 132, 174
pests, 174
petroglyphs, **17**, 162
Phalaris, 65
pharmacopoeia, natural, 89
Phoenicians, 90
Phoenix dactylifera, 149
physic garden, **90**, **91**
Piermont, Dennis, 109
pincushion flower, **65**
pine, 62, 149
pineapple shrub, **129**
pine-scented thyme, 126-127
pink, symbolism of, 32
Pinus contorta, 101
Pinus densiflora, 101
plane tree, 49
plantain lily, 33
plants, spiritual language of, 57-62
plants, toxic, 94
Platanus occidentalis, 64
Pliny, 40
poet's jessamine, **61**
poke (plant), 72
pollination, 65
Polygonatum odoratum, 87
pomegranate, 148
ponds, **39**, 81, **85**, 105, 149, 172
poplar, 62
pot marigold, 95
prairie, 118
prairie dock, 45
prairie grasses, 119
Prairie Nursery (Westfield, Wisconsin), 116
propagation (see also seed-saving), 175-177
Prunus sargentii, 179
Prunus triloba, 179
Psalms, Book of, 18, 41, 146, 147, 148, 152
purification, ritual, 109
purple coneflower, **93**, 95, **128**
purple, symbolism of, 30-32
pyrethrin, 175

Q
queen of the meadow, 126

R
Ra, 65, 90

Raikyu-ji Temple garden, 104
Ramses III, 40
rectangle, symbolism of, 49
red oak, 148
red, symbolism of, 29
Reed, Douglas, 96
Reflections of the Spirit, 110
Renaissance, concept of garden during, 15
Resurrection, 153, 177
Revelations, Book of, 145
Rhea, 113
ribbon-grass, 65
Rigveda, 93
rijo, 109
Rikyu, 111, 166
Rikyu, Sen no, 107
Riordan, Richard, 71
rock, symbolism of (see also stone), 104, 105, **108**
rock, use in the Zen garden, 101, **105**
Rodef Shalom Biblical Botanical Garden, **144**, 148-149, **149**
roji, 108
Rome, ancient, 15, 40
Rosa canina, 153
Rosa carolina, 153
Rosa gallica, **94**
Rosa 'Ruby Wedding', **61**
Rosa rugosa, 153
rose, 32, 57, 120, 122, 126, 128, 152
rose of Sharon, 83, 118, 148
Rose, Jeanne, 124
rose, symbolism of, 59-61
rosemary, 40, 51, 95, 148
Rosmarinus officinalis, 51, 95
rowan, 140, 142
Rudbeckia, 65
Rudolf Steiner Fellowship Foundation garden, 92
Rudolf Steiner Fellowship Foundation, 118
rue, 64, 94, 148
Russian sage, 126, **128**
Ruta graveolens, 64, 94
Ruth (biblical), 149

S
sacred space, creating outdoors, 11, 20-25
sacred space, definition of, 10
saffron crocus, 178

sage, 33, 51, 147, 148, 149, 154
saint's gardens, 150-155
saints, flowers symbolic of, 51
salvia, 51, **128**, 147
Salvia dominica, 147
Salvia officinalis, 33
Salvia officinalis, 'Icterina', 51
Salvia palaestina, 147
Salvia purpurea, 51
San Francisco Zen Center, **117**
santolina, 120
Santostefano, Sebastiano, Dr. 96
Sarton, May, 11, 15, 86
satori, 107
Satsong (Petaluma, California), **157**
Scabiosa atropurpurea, 65
scent, 40, 83, 178
Scented Garden, The, 41
Scotland, labyrinths in, 163
Scully, Vincent, 159
sculpture (see also statuary), 45, **133**
Sea of Galilee, 149
seasons, 41
seating, 119
Second Coming, 179
seed, symbolic meaning of, 12
seed-saving (see also propagation), 114, 122, 175-177
senses, use of in garden design, 77
shade, use of in the garden, 143
shaman, 90
shamrock, 143
Shimizu, Osamu, 168
Shintoism, 20, 99, 101, 104
Shiva, 40, 90
shore pine, **42**, 101
Shoyoan Teien, 100
shrines, 101
shrines, Shinto, 109
shumisen104
Siberian dogwood, 86
Silphium terebinthinaceum, 45
Simpson, Missy, 118
Simpson, Tommy, 118, 172
'Sioux Blue' Indian grass, 45

Sioux, 113
skullcap (herb), 72
Slawson, David, 171
smell, sense of, 124, 125
Smith, Lillian, 157
snowdrop, **58**, 152
snow-on-the-mountain, 84-85
soil, 68, 174
soil amendments, 174
soil-testing, 174
Sojo, 107
Solomon, 145
Solomon's seal, 87
Sonenberg, Fred, 76-77
Song of Solomon, 147, 152, 179
Sorghastrum nutans, 'Sioux Blue', 45
Sorghum bicolor, 149
sound, symbolism of, 153
sound, use of in the garden, 137
spearmint, 64
speedwell, 72
spider, 67, **67**
spray paint, 157
spruce, 62
square, symbolism of, 49
squirreltail grass, **35**
St. John's Episcopal Church (Montclair, New Jersey), 160
St. John's wort, 95
St. Paul's Episcopal Church, 51
Stachys byzantina, 26
star of Bethlehem, 148
Staten Island Botanical Garden, **130**
statuary (see also sculpture), 76, **112**, 119, 136, 137, **137**, 143, 151, 154, 169
stepping stones, **55**
steps and stairs, 52-55, **56**
sternbergia, 149
stewardship, 68, 69, 116, 117, 152
Stokesia laevis, 26
stone, use of in garden design (see also rock), 46, 80
storax, 148
strawberry, 118
streams, 149
stroll gardens, 55, **98**, 99
Sukkoth, 149
Sumeria, 40
sun god, 141
sun, symbolism of, 41-42
sunflower, **59**, 61, 64, **114**, 153

sweet rocket, 126
sweet William, 153
sweetgrass, 72
switch grass, 45
sycamore, 49, 64
symbolic landscape, creating, 45-55
Symphytum officinale, 92

T
Tagetes patula, 63
Tagore, Rabindranath, 129
Tai Chi, 134, 135, 136
Tammuz, 59
Taoism, 99, 105, 132
Taoist garden, 19
Taraxacum officinale, 64, 92, 149
taro, 83
Tarot, 120
Taxus baccata, **62**
Taxus cuspidata, 84, 170
tea, 108
tea ceremony, 109
tea gardens, **19**, 55
teahouse, 109
teahouse garden, 99, 108
Tecophilaea cyanocrocus, 30, **31**
temples, Buddhist, 109
Ten Commandments, 146
Teucrium chamaedrys, 50
Tewa, 162
therapy, gardening as, 24-25
Thompson, Nancy, 148
Thoreau, Henry David, 175
Three Sisters, 63
thresholds, symbolism of, 55
Thuja occidentalis, 84, 170
thyme, 51, **124**, **127**, 127
Thymus caespititius, 127
Thymus camphoratus, 127
Thymus x citriodorus, 127
Thymus herba-barona, 127
Thymus pseudolanuginosis, 127
time, 41-45
tobacco plant, **128**
tobacco, ornamental, 126
torii, 104
tranquillity garden, 79-88
Transcendentalists, 44
transitional areas, 55-56
traps, pest, 175
Tree of Life, 47, 61, 62, 149, 158
tree spirits, 140
trees, symbolism of, 57-62

Treesinger, Jaen, 76, 89, 128
triangle, symbolism of, 49
Trinity, 27, 57, 71
trumpet vine, 62, 117
trumpet-creeper, 153
Tsuga canadensis, **26**
tulip, 148
two-winged silverbells, 44

U-V
urn-fruited eucalyptus, **27**
Vayu, 37
Vedas, 93
vegetable garden, 120, 137
Venus, 28, 59, 120
Verey, Rosemary, 41
Versailles, gardens at, 15
Viburnum lentago, **29**
viburnum, 153
vines, 61-62, 86-87, 143
Vinyard, Jan, 117
Virgin Mary, 20, 30, 51, 58, 61, 66, 147, 151, 152, 179
Virgin Mary (statuary), **150, 152, 154**
Virgin's bower, 152
Vishnu, 30, 58
Vitarka Mudra, **21**
von Arnim, Countess, 165

W
Walking a Sacred Path, 52
walkways (see also paths), 51, 157
wall germander, 50
Warsaw Biblical Garden (Indiana), 148-149
water features, **109**, 118, 136, 143, 154, **167, 171**, 171-172
water lily 81, **85**, 118, 148, **149**, 171, 172
water sprites, 139
water, symbolism of, 37, **132**
water, use of in the garden, 82, 111
waterfalls, 149
waterfalls, symbolism of, **104**
Waverly Abbey, **62**
web of life, 66, 69, 117, 143
Webb, Mary, 27
weeping mulberry, 148
weeping willow, 118
white, symbolism of, 28-29
Whittier, John Greenleaf, 49

Wilder, Louise Bebbe, 32
wildflowers, 115, 116, 119
wildlife, 52, 65-69, 117, 118, 119, 137, 153
willow, 62, 142, 149
wind (in the garden), 80
wind, symbolism of, 36
winter honeysuckle, 153
winterberry, 153
winter hazel, 179
wisteria, 122
witch hazel, 72, 179
witchcraft, 142
wood, symbolism of, 49, 140
wood, use of in the garden, 46, 47
Woods, Pamela, 76, 119-120, 135
woolly thyme, 127
World of the Japanese Garden, The, 107
world tree, 142
wormwood, 33, 122, 146, 148

Y
yarrow, 92, 116
Yeats, William Butler, 139
Yellow Emperor's Classic, The, 93
yellow flag, 149
yellow, symbolism of, 29
yew, 62
Yezierska, Anzia, 67
yin and yang, 19, 35, 100, 132, 154, 137
yogas, 93
Yun, Lin, 134

Z
Zacharia, Book of, 147
zazen, 81
Zea mays, 92
zebra grass, 37, 83
Zen gardens, 20, 37, 41, 46, 70, 70, 83, 98-111
Zen Mountain Monastery (Mt. Tremper, New York), **107, 169**
Zeohrer, 44-45
Zeus, 30, 113, 115

SOURCES OF QUOTATIONS

Throughout the pages of this book, we have quoted the words of other writers; following is a list of the writers and their works, from which the quotations are drawn.

William Longgood, *Voices from the Earth: A Year in the Life of A Garden.* New York: W.W. Norton & Company, 1991.

May Sarton, quoted in *A Gardener's Bouquet of Quotations,* edited by Maria Polushkin Robbins. Hopewell, New Jersey: The Ecco Press, 1993.

Charles Dudley Warner, quoted in *A Gardener's Bouquet of Quotations.*

Mary Webb, *The Joy of Spring,* 1917..

John Greenleaf Whittier, "To Charles Sumner"

Anzia Yezerierska, *Red Ribbon on a White Horse,* 1917.

Lao Tzu, from *Tao te Ching,* edited by Peg Streep. Boston: Bulfinch Press, 1994.

Mirabel Osler, *In the Eye of the Garden.* New York: Macmillan Publishing Company, 1993.

Thomas Merton, *Seeds of Contemplation.* New Directions Publishing Company, 1949.

May Sarton, *Journal of a Solitude.* New York: W.W. Norton, 1973.

Hippocrites, *Regime in Health*

Sioux and Zuni poems from *The Sacred Journey: Prayers and Songs of Native America,* edited by Peg Streep. Boston: Bulfinch Press.

Edna St. Vincent Millay, "Renascence," from *Renascence,* 1917.

William Butler Yeats, from "Fergus and the Druid," from *The Rose,* 1893.

Elizabeth Barrett Browning, "Aurora Leigh"

Lillian Smith, *The Journey,* 1954.

Countess Van Arnim,.*Elizabeth and Her German Garden*

Rachel Carson, *The Sense of Wonder,* 1954.

Anne Morrow Lindbergh, *A Gift from the Sea.* New York: Pantheon Books, 1955

GARDEN DESIGN CREDITS

Dr. Alex Champion: pp. 10 bottom, 156, 158, 161, 163
Tim Brown: p. 54
Pat Cook: p. 10, top right
Filoli Gardens: pp. 55, 72.
Chris Jacobson: pp. 48, 56 right, 71, 117, 156 right.
Jeff Lee: pp. 20, 108 right
Michael Miller: p. 47
Stephen Morrell: pp. 47 top; 19, 98, 105 (Hume Stroll Garden); 42, 101 right (Shoyoan Teien).
Schedel Gardens, Elmore, Ohio: p. 104
David Slawson: pp. 101, 105, 167, 169
Leigh Sorenson: p. 104
Chris Wood, Chanticleer: pp. 85 right, 80 left
Additional credits in captions.

ILLUSTRATION CREDITS

Illustrations on pp. 134, 160 © Claudia Karabaic Sargent

All photos © **John Glover** except for the following:

©**Ian Adams,** pp. 23, 24, 26 left, 30 right, 49 right, 50, 54 left, 56 bottom right, 90, 100 left; 101, 102, 103 bottom, 109 right, 129 right, 138, 140 left, 144, 146 top, 147, 148 right, 149 (both), 167 left, 167 bottom, 169 right, 171, 172 left, 176
©**Noella Barringer,** pp. 66 right, 95, 109 left, 136 right, 139
©**Whit Bronaugh,** pp. 14, 38 left
©**Rick Darke,** p. 44 (both)
©**Larry Hansen,** p. 110 far left
©**Bill Keogh,** pp. 70, 131, 133 (both), 137
©**Donna DeMari,** pp. 88, 167 right
©**William Dewey,** pp. 18, 60 left, 78
©**Maggie Oster:** pp. 37, 38 right, 40, 46 right, 128 left, 153
©**Cindy A. Pavlinac, Sacred Land Photography:** pp. 17, bottom, 41 left
©**Leonard Phillips:** pp. 10, top left, 20, 84, 108 right
©**Dianne Pratt:** p. 111
©**Steven Sharnoff:** p. 116
©**Albert Squillace:** pp. 10 top right, 26 right, 27 left, 29 right, 57 left, 60 right, 93 center, 110 right

Acknowledgments

First, many thanks to Claudia Karabaic Sargent for her friendship and help. Many people were kind enough to share their expertise, their personal experiences of spiritual gardening, and their gardens for photography, both with me and Lori Stein of Layla Productions. Heartfelt thanks to one and all. Work becomes a richer experience by the connection to like-minded people, among them: Rev. E. Michael Allen, Cam Allen, Jenee Areeckel, Robin Rose Bennett, Nancy Blair, Liz Bossa, Lois Brown, Penelope Byham, Marty Cain, Jo Carson, Alex Champion, Laura Chester, Dr. Jennifer Choate, Reverand Diana Clark, Pat Cook, Thomas Bachellor Cox, Helen Curry, Brenda Corey, Davy Dabney, Rick Darke, Christy Dennis, James Desurra, Anne Dewey, Neil Diboll, Bill Enoch, Ann Evans, Audrey Flack, Kristina Flanaghan, Maria Gabaldo, Diane Garisto, Leslie Garisto, Mary Gerken, Tessa Gowans, James Heaton III, Paul Heimbach, Sonia Hodson, Donna Hopper, Stephen Huyler, Irene Jacob, Chris Jacobson, Wendy Johnson, Bill Johnston, E. Barrie Kavasch, Marcia and Jack Kelly, Kevin Koga, Dennis Kurutz, Jane Lahr, Joan Larned, Cynthia Lawton, Jeff Lee, Kate Learson, Mark Leuchten, Jami Lin, Karen Lukas, Dan Lurie, Tovah Martin, Michado Meade, Jeff Mendoza, Emil Miland, Tibol Miller, Stephen Morrell, Maggie Oster, Sukie Parmalee, Cindy Pavlinac, Mr. and Mrs. Penick, Dennis Piermont, David Pryor, Tom Rogers, Jeanne Rose, Father Joseph Ryan, Dr. Sebastiano Santostefano, Noah Schwartz, Brother Allred Seeton, Danielle Seltzer, Simon Shelmerdine, Holly and Osamu Shimizu, Tommy and Missy Simpson, Sr. Maureen Skelly, Fred Sonenberg, Deb Soule, Leigh Sorenson, Deena Stein, Michelle Stein, Mary Lou Taylor, Sarah Teofanov, Nancy Thompson, Jaen Treesinger, Takeo Uesugi, Bonnie Lane Webber, Chris Woods, Pamela Woods, Etti Yammer, and Gabrielle Young

Many thanks too to the talented photographers whose work graces these pages: John Glover, principal photographer, and Ian Adams, Noella Barringer, Whit Bronaugh, Donna DeMari, Rick Darke, Bill Dewey, Bill Keogh, Maggie Oster, Cindy Pavlinac, Leonard Phillips, Diane Pratt, Steven Sharnoff, and Albert Squillace. And special thanks to our designer, Annemarie Redmond, whose work shows these pictures to their best advantage.

The team at Time Life, too, deserves credit: Anna Burgard, an editor like no other, helped an idea for a book become a book, as did Neil Levin, Jennifer Pearce, and Laura McNeill.

And, finally, a big thank you to the best child in the world. You know who you are.